# POLICEWOMEN
# WHO MADE
# HISTORY

# POLICEWOMEN WHO MADE HISTORY

**Breaking Through the Ranks**

**Robert L. Snow**

Rowman & Littlefield Publishers, Inc.
Lanham • Boulder • New York • Toronto • Plymouth, UK

Published by Rowman & Littlefield Publishers, Inc.
A wholly owned subsidiary of
The Rowman & Littlefield Publishing Group, Inc.
4501 Forbes Boulevard, Suite 200, Lanham, Maryland 20706
http://www.rowmanlittlefield.com

Estover Road, Plymouth PL6 7PY, United Kingdom

British Library Cataloguing in Publication Information Available

**Library of Congress Cataloging-in-Publication Data**

Snow, Robert L.
  Policewomen who made history : breaking through the ranks / Robert L.
Snow.
      p. cm.
  Includes bibliographical references.
  ISBN 978-1-4422-0033-3 (cloth : alk. paper)— ISBN 978-1-4422-0035-7
(electronic)
  1. Policewomen—United States. 2. Policewomen—United States—History.
I. Title.
  HV8023.S66 2010
  363.2092'273—dc22                              2009048664

∞™ The paper used in this publication meets the minimum requirements of
American National Standard for Information Sciences—Permanence of Paper
for Printed Library Materials, ANSI/NISO Z39.48-1992.

Printed in the United States of America

## DEDICATION

To Alan's New Crew:
Alicia, Nolan, Lexi, and Little Alan
Welcome to the family!


*In Memory:*
Elizabeth Coffal Robinson
May 10, 1942–April 8, 2009

Betty Campbell Blankenship
July 18, 1934–March 18, 2002

# CONTENTS

# FOREWORD

In 2003, when I headed the Indianapolis Police Department's Homicide Branch, I received a call one evening that an Indianapolis police officer had been shot. Naturally, I went to the scene not only to be certain that my detectives had all of the resources they needed to carry out a complete investigation, but also to be a conduit of information to the chief of police and his staff, who would need to know the details of what had happened.

When I got to the scene, the lead detective filled me in on what had occurred. A man had apparently committed an armed robbery, and then fled from the scene in a car. Moments later, several uniformed officers had spotted the car and attempted to stop it. After a short chase, the suspect crashed his car, but then, rather than surrendering, he came out of the car with an assault rifle and began firing at the officers who had pursued him, striking one of them. Fortunately, the lead detective told me, the wound to the officer, though serious, wasn't fatal. Then, in his routine recital of facts, the lead detective told me something else. The officer wounded by the assault rifle fire had been a policewoman.

Later that night, I thought about the incident, and about how much had changed since I became a police officer in the late 1960s. In September 1968, just months before the city swore me in as a police officer,

Indianapolis had become the first city in the United States to assign a two-officer team of policewomen, Liz Coffal and Betty Blankenship, to street patrol, and there had been quite a row about it then, but no one gave much thought any longer to seeing uniformed policewomen driving police cars or seeing policewomen as detectives. Policewomen today routinely handle the same jobs as men, and share the same risks. A decade before the shooting incident described here, we had already lost a policewoman killed in the line of duty. Things had certainly changed.

A few years later, my wife and I, while on vacation, stopped to see the National Police Memorial in Washington, D.C. Afterward, we walked over to the gift shop. Along the top border of the walls of the gift shop someone had painted a time chart of the important events in the history of American policing. My wife, who had been a policewoman with the Indianapolis Police Department for twenty-four years, noticed a glaring omission. The chart contained no mention in 1968 of policewomen first being assigned to street patrol, this despite the fact that the memorial to slain police officers we had just visited had several hundred policewomen honored on it. My wife was incensed at this oversight, not only because she had been a policewoman, but also because she and Liz Coffal were best friends. When my wife got home she began an e-mail and telephone campaign to have this oversight corrected.

I, too, felt a bit surprised that the people at the National Police Memorial could overlook such a crucial date in American policing. So I checked with several sources that dealt with the history of American policing and found that the ones that did mention it gave the event in 1968 only a sentence or two, and at best a paragraph. That too surprised me, because anyone familiar with the history of American policing knows that, following the success of the Indianapolis program, American policing radically changed forever. What had once been a male-only occupation suddenly became a wide open field of opportunity for women. Following Liz's and Betty's demonstration that women could do the job of street patrol as well as men, police departments no longer confined policewomen to just minor jobs at police headquarters, but instead policewomen began branching out into virtually every area of police work.

I wondered just how many people in our country didn't know about the history of policewomen, about their humble beginnings and about how far they have come since 1968. I suspected that if the people who run the National Police Memorial, which contains the names of several hundred slain policewomen, didn't seem to be aware of it, then few members of the public were likely aware of it either.

While I had already decided to write this book, the event in Washington, D.C., made me even more certain of its necessity. I believed I needed to show readers how the position of policewomen came about in the United States, and how for almost one hundred years policewomen have fought a hard and often bitter battle for equality with policemen. I felt I needed to show how, though once relegated to only "safe" jobs within police headquarters, many policewomen insisted on being allowed to take the same risks as policemen, to stand shoulder to shoulder with their brother officers in the fight against crime. I wanted to show readers the great contributions women have made to law enforcement, and how much law enforcement has gained through accepting policewomen as equals. I hope this book does that.

# ● 1

# THE MOMENT

Liz Coffal's hand trembled just enough so that the car key she was holding moved noticeably. Since early that morning, her stomach had been filled with electricity, but now that the moment had at last arrived, the voltage seemed to be surging at full power, rippling out her arms and fingertips. As she got into the police car, a 1964 black-and-white Ford Custom with Indianapolis Police Department emblems on the doors and red lights and siren on the roof, Liz's breath hitched in her chest. The moment was here at last.

"I had wanted this for so long," Liz said, "but when the moment finally arrived, it was really scary."[1]

Next to her, in the passenger seat, sat fellow policewoman thirty-four-year-old Betty Blankenship, eight years Liz's senior. Betty didn't look to Liz as though she was faring any better. Liz could see perspiration on Betty's upper lip.

Liz and Betty were about to do something that had never been done before in the United States. They were going to make history. Two big-city policewomen were getting ready to go out in a police car on street patrol, a totally male-dominated job for as long as America had been a country.

"We knew we were making history," Liz said, "but the size and scope of what we were doing didn't really occur to us until years later. At the moment, we just wanted to show that we could do the same nitty-gritty work that the men did."[2]

It was September 10, 1968, and Liz and Betty, dressed in Indianapolis Police Department blue jackets and skirts, their guns in their purses, were headed out into hostile territory. If reality turned out to be anything like their dreams, they would be going on dangerous radio runs, where the people they would deal with would often be angry, drunk or high, and occasionally violent.

Liz and Betty, both strikingly attractive women who many of the male officers had flirted with, realized they couldn't count on that type of male attention any longer. Instead, they knew they would likely receive little, if any, support from the other street officers they would be working with. The male officers had made no secret of the fact that they resented women attempting to enter their domain. No policewoman in a major city in the United States had ever done this before because, according to the men who controlled access to the job, the work was just too dangerous, too physically demanding, and too raw and uncivilized for a woman.

Because the men in control felt this way, policewomen in the United States had always been relegated to certain "safe" jobs within a police department. Once out of the training academy, policewomen could look forward to working the remainder of their careers as jail matrons, juvenile officers, or perhaps as a secretary to one of the high-ranking senior police officers. (Often these high-ranking officers would handle extremely sensitive information or material that needed to be transcribed or put into memos and letters. Due to its sensitive nature, this information and material, police departments felt, should be handled only by police officers. Consequently, police departments often recruited policewomen specifically to work as secretaries.) But street patrol? Taking radio runs in a police car? Certainly not. That was, and always had been, absolutely off-limits to policewomen. But that was about to change. The moment had come.

After several tries, Liz finally got the car key into the ignition. She held her breath again for a moment. What would she and Betty face today? Would all of their detractors be right, or would they be able to handle whatever they came across?

Yes! Yes, they would be able to handle it, Liz told herself. She and Betty had fought too long for this moment not to believe they would succeed. Still, both women knew that almost all of the male officers on the police department, with the exception perhaps of the chief of police, whom they had persuaded to give them the chance to do this, felt absolutely certain they would fail. Practically every male officer on the police department thought that this was just a cockamamie idea by a new, young, idealistic chief that would explode in his face. It would never work.

≪

Before 1968, no major city in the United States had given the idea of policewomen on street patrol any really serious consideration. Even though the President's Commission on Law Enforcement and the Administration of Justice had stated in their report of 1967, "Their value should not be considered as limited to staff functions or police work with juveniles; women should also serve regularly in patrol, vice, and investigative functions,"[3] few police administrators gave the possibility of policewomen on uniformed street patrol any really serious thought.

Historically, police administrators hadn't considered putting policewomen on street patrol because no one could argue that uniformed police patrol wasn't a physically demanding job that many times required considerable upper body strength. Police officers often had to carry injured people out of dangerous and hazardous environments, break down doors, chase criminals, and many times subdue these criminals physically. The accepted belief was that women simply weren't physically equipped to do these things.

But just as much a reason for not putting policewomen on street patrol was the danger factor. Street work for police officers is undeniably dangerous. Street officers routinely interact with angry, hostile people. They also come in daily contact with extremely dangerous criminals. A glance at any memorial a police department has erected to its officers killed in the line of duty clearly shows that the large majority of these

slain officers are uniformed street officers. It's the most dangerous job
in the department.

In addition to the danger, street officers also see the absolute worst
side of humanity. They daily see example after example of humanity's
depravity and cruelty. The work simply isn't fit for women, or so the
belief had been ever since New York City hired the first women to work
as jail matrons in 1845.

In May 1957, however, a man named Winston Churchill joined the
Indianapolis Police Department. Given a historically significant name at
birth, Churchill apparently felt pressured by the fame of his namesake
to go beyond the ordinary, and to make his mark by doing something
extraordinary. In 1968, he did just that.

For several years before joining the Indianapolis Police Department,
Churchill, who had planned on a career in teaching, owned a wrecker
lot. As the owner, he often came in contact with police officers who had
cars towed there. He would listen to their seemingly never-ending stories
about police work and its excitement. Eventually, being a teacher didn't
seem to hold much of a thrill any longer. Churchill could also sense that
these officers felt they were really doing something good for the world,
that in a small way they knew they were making a difference. After several years, Churchill finally decided that teaching wasn't his calling after
all, and he applied to join the Indianapolis Police Department.

The police department accepted Churchill, and, in May 1957, he entered as a recruit officer. As all male officers did then, following recruit
training, Churchill found himself assigned to street patrol. He served as
a uniformed officer answering citizen calls until 1962 when the department promoted him to detective and reassigned him to the Burglary
and Larceny Branch. In 1964, Churchill passed the sergeant's exam, and
the department promoted him. Then, in 1968, the police department
promoted him again, this time to the rank of lieutenant.

Between promotions, though, and following his stint as a burglary
and larceny detective, Churchill received an assignment to the police
department training academy, where he served as an instructor. Since
he had a love of education, this spot seemed to be a perfect fit for him.
While the Indianapolis Police Department Training Academy routinely
handled the continuing in-service training for its officers, its main job
consisted of instructing new recruits.

For most of its history, the Indianapolis Police Department had recruited policewomen, though usually in very small numbers compared with their male counterparts. Although there were only certain jobs within the department that these women could be assigned to, policewomen still received the same training at the academy as the male officers. They learned criminal law, arrest and detention procedures, defensive tactics, and how to shoot a gun.

In 1967, two policewomen in a recruit class Churchill taught, Elizabeth Coffal and Betty Blankenship, began talking to him about the restriction against policewomen being assigned to police cars on street patrol. They argued that they didn't think it was fair, and should be changed. Policewomen could do the job, they told him, just in a different way than men.

Churchill had already thought about this, and he felt they were right. "I felt that having women police in the department was not fair to the department," Churchill told me. "It was not fair because they were getting the same wage and benefits as the men, but they worked only in minor, safe jobs. They weren't providing the department with nearly the energy or productivity of the men.

"But," Churchill added, "it also wasn't fair to the women. Policewomen were stuck either in the juvenile aid office or in secretarial spots, with their chances for promotion seriously hampered. Their future in the department was dramatically denied."[4]

Although Churchill didn't envision policewomen as being no different from male officers, he did believe that women had certain strengths and abilities that men didn't. These strengths and abilities, he felt, could be very useful on street patrol.

"If you compare the qualities of what makes a good policeman and a good policewoman, many of the qualities are duplicated," Churchill told me. "But many are not. Women can often be more perceptive than men. Women can often pick up details that men miss. If a man, for example, says that a car is red, and a woman says it's burgundy, you can believe it's burgundy. Women are also often more intuitive than men, and women can many times get witnesses to open up when men can't.

"My vision, though, was not to squeeze women into the same mold as their male counterparts, which is what we see today. Today, policewomen must dress like and act like a man in order to be accepted. My vision was to instead allow policewomen to have their own mold, and to use their special talents to benefit the police department.

"But today we seem to want to back away from nurturing these qualities that would make women excel as police officers, and instead mold them into what society apparently thinks they should be—a duplicate of a policeman. It's such a waste of talent."[5]

Yes, Churchill agreed when Liz and Betty talked to him about it, policewomen should be given the opportunity to go on street patrol. He told Liz and Betty that if he was ever named chief of police to come back and see him, and he would put them on street patrol.

In 1967, Indianapolis had been a Democratic stronghold for many years, with Democratic mayors controlling city hall and consequently the police department. That November, however, a brash newcomer to the political scene, thirty-six-year-old Republican Richard G. Lugar, whose only office before this had been on the school board, won the race for mayor of Indianapolis. Since the Democrats had been in charge of the city for many years, they had always selected the police chief and his command staff from Democratic loyalists within the police department. Now there was going to be a change.

Richard Lugar put out a notice that he would interview anyone in the police department with the rank of lieutenant or above (as state law required) who was interested in being the chief of police or one of the other six appointed ranks (assistant chief, deputy chiefs, and inspectors). Since Churchill didn't have any strong political connections in Indianapolis when he signed up for an interview, something all former chiefs had needed, he didn't really expect to be named chief of police, but rather hoped for one of the smaller appointed spots, perhaps as an inspector. He figured that becoming chief was still a number of years away. He knew, though, that if he could get one of the lesser-appointed ranks, then he would be able to show what he could do, and eventually advance to the office of chief of police.

"When Dick Lugar became mayor, I knew he would make seven appointments within the police department," Churchill said. "But I didn't know Lugar. Had never met the man. I also had no political connections. So I felt that chief of police was probably out of the question. I was just hoping to get any one of the other six spots."[6]

For his interview, Churchill prepared a detailed plan of what he thought ought to be done at the Indianapolis Police Department in order to bring it up to where he believed it should be for the late 1960s. When called for his interview, Churchill presented his plan for the department, and his thirty-minute interview lasted for an hour and forty minutes. He left the interview feeling good, believing that perhaps one of the minor appointed spots might be his.

Several days later, Churchill received a call from the chairman of the interview board, who said that Mayor Lugar wanted him to come out to his house that night at nine o'clock for a meeting. Still hoping for one of the lesser jobs, Churchill expected to find six other cars parked at Lugar's house.

"I thought if there were only six cars there, then I was in," Churchill said. "But when I got to the mayor's house, there were no other cars there."[7]

The meeting, as it turned out, would be just between Churchill and the mayor. He and Lugar sat down and discussed Churchill's vision for the police department until three in the morning. Even with that, however, Lugar told Churchill that he couldn't commit just yet, but that he would hear from him soon. At ten o'clock the next morning, Lugar called Churchill and told him that he had the job as chief, and to be in his office at noon with some prepared words to say.

Reeling from the unexpected show of confidence Lugar had given him and his vision, Churchill immediately began to implement his plans for changing the Indianapolis Police Department. During his near seven years as chief of police, Churchill instituted a number of groundbreaking programs that other police departments would soon begin to imitate, such as the take-home car program, the college incentive program, the citizen ride-along program, and many others. But his biggest, most controversial, and most historical program would begin after Liz and Betty went to see him as chief in order to remind him of his promise to them.

"I didn't think about it as being a historical decision," Churchill told me. "Instead, I thought about how valuable it would be to the city, and to the women, too. It would be good for them and good for us, so let's do it. And even for those women who didn't choose to go out onto the street, they still knew that the opportunity was there. The door was now open."[8]

So, Churchill made good on his promise, and soon every other police chief in the nation was watching Indianapolis intently and nervously to see what would happen. Many expected, and perhaps hoped, that the program would fail, but still they watched Indianapolis closely because they knew that, if the program succeeded, then the pressure would be on them to do the same thing.

"I didn't really think that much at first about the ramifications if the program didn't work, if the women, or someone else, had been unnecessarily hurt or some other catastrophe had happened," Churchill said. "I did later, though, when an incident came up where the women had to pull their guns on some guy. A lot of people were upset. There was a big flap about it. The idea of a policewoman pulling her weapon on a man! It was unheard of. But, hey, I told everyone, that's just part of police work."[9]

≫

Liz finally started the police car and pulled it out of the basement parking garage of the City-County Building in downtown Indianapolis, where the police department had its headquarters. Betty picked up the radio microphone and told the dispatchers that Car 47 was ready to take runs.

What would follow this moment would be much different from what Liz and Betty had imagined. They would soon find themselves, although making history, also facing obstacles and problems they had never expected.

Liz and Betty would make their mark that day in 1968, and forever change the face of American policing. In the coming chapters we will discuss Liz and Betty and the many changes they brought about, but first we will look at the 123 years that led up to Liz's and Betty's breakthrough.

# 2

# HISTORY OF WOMEN
# IN POLICING, 1845–1968

On April 7, 1922, a Washington, D.C., Police Department trial board cleared police lieutenant Mina Van Winkle of the charge of insubordination. Lieutenant Van Winkle at that time held the position of commander of the Women's Bureau of the Washington, D.C., Police Department. She also headed the International Policewomen's Association, and had become one of the top success stories in the world when it came to policewomen. Many observers of the trial felt that the proceedings didn't have as much to do with any wrongdoing on the part of Lieutenant Van Winkle as it did with certain individuals wanting to strike a blow at the idea of women invading the centuries-old, male-only domain of police work.

The case against Lieutenant Van Winkle came about because, on February 25, 1922, the Washington, D.C., chief of police issued an order stating, "All matters relating to cases of lost children and cases of females of whatever age found wandering abroad and unable to give proper account of themselves and against whom no charge is to be placed will be handled by the Women's Bureau exclusively and not by the Detective Bureau, as heretofore."[1]

On March 20, 1922, two young girls, one fourteen and the other fifteen, ran away from their homes in New York City, eventually ending up in Washington, D.C. After several days, the two girls, having no money and nowhere to stay, telegraphed their fathers in New York City for help. The fathers immediately notified the Washington, D.C., Police Department, and the Detective Bureau dispatched two detectives, in violation of the chief's recent order, to Union Station to pick up the girls. The detectives, again in violation of the chief's order, took the two girls to the Detective Bureau and questioned them extensively. It wasn't until 1:30 in the morning that the detectives finally delivered the two girls to the custody of the Women's Bureau.

The two fathers, apparently anxious for the safety of their daughters, caught a midnight train from New York City to Washington. D.C. After a stop at the Detective Bureau, the two fathers showed up at the Women's Bureau and demanded that the two girls be released to them. Reportedly, they had been assured at the Detective Bureau that they would get immediate custody.

A worker at the Women's Bureau called Lieutenant Van Winkle and asked her what she should do. This was the first time Lieutenant Van Winkle heard about the two runaway girls. The worker told Lieutenant Van Winkle that an inspector from the Detective Bureau had just called her and ordered her to release the two girls to the men, which, as it turned out, he didn't really have the authority to do.

Lieutenant Van Winkle called the inspector and said that before she could release the girls, she first had to be certain that the two men were actually the girls' fathers, something the Detective Bureau had apparently failed to verify. The inspector said okay, that was fine with him.

As it turned out, the two fathers had to wait several hours before the Women's Bureau finally released their daughters, which infuriated the two men as the Detective Bureau had apparently assured them the girls would be released with no delay. Reportedly, one of the fathers was well-connected politically and raised such a furor with his political connections that the police department brought Lieutenant Van Winkle up on charges of insubordination.

Interestingly, no charges were brought, or apparently even considered, against the members of the Detective Bureau who started the whole incident by taking the two girls to their office and questioning them until well after midnight, in violation of the police chief's orders. If they had followed the chief's orders and let the Women's Bureau take custody of the girls from the start, the event likely wouldn't have reached the extremes it did.

The trial board exonerated Lieutenant Van Winkle, but, amazingly, added that she "did not appear to have a proper conception of the cardinal principle of discipline."[2] This puzzled everyone who knew anything about the case, since Lieutenant Van Winkle had followed proper procedure throughout. Most likely, many connected with the case thought, this was simply a concession to the two fathers. Also, in its findings, the trial board didn't mention the actions of the members of the Detective Bureau.

This obviously unwarranted attack on Lieutenant Van Winkle was not the first she had suffered. As one of the first high-ranking policewomen in the history of the United States, she had been the target of a number of attacks by individuals and organizations that vigorously opposed the intrusion of women into policing, which had been a male-only domain for centuries. An article about Lieutenant Van Winkle from 1922 stated, "Washingtonians have observed that one of this city's newspapers has consistently endeavored to make hard sledding for her administration ever since it started."[3]

It should be apparent to readers from this anecdote that Lieutenant Van Winkle and other policewomen of her day didn't have an easy road during their careers. Many citizens, both men and women, vigorously opposed the idea of introducing women into the field of policing. And, like the trumped-up charge against Lieutenant Van Winkle, they did everything they could to derail the growing trend across the United States to hire women as police officers.

A big part of the problem was that the widespread employment of policewomen across our nation began at nearly the same time that the Suffrage Movement reached its height. Many people saw women's suffrage as portending the end of the world as they knew it, and they often saw the intrusion of policewomen into the profession in the same way. Many individuals in the United States saw these events as radical changes to a way of life they wanted to maintain, and they were prepared to fight these changes with all of their strength and will.

For a number of years, one of the major arguments against police-women, besides the commonly held belief that "a woman's place is in the home," was the belief that hiring policewomen would bring about "race suicide." By this, detractors insisted that if women were allowed to seek long-term employment outside the home, then they would not want to get married and have children, and consequently the population would shrink drastically.

In answer to this argument, in the March 31, 1907, issue of the *New York Times,* Julia Goldzier, an ardent supporter of the idea of police-women, states, "The horrified public shouts that policewomen would encourage race suicide. . . . Is not one child saved equal to one born?" Mrs. Goldzier then goes on to talk about how policewomen, through their actions, could save the lives of many children, lives that would be lost otherwise. She ends by saying, "Policewomen would be daily and hourly performing such deeds, so they would do more than any one mother toward preventing race suicide."[4]

The anecdote involving Lieutenant Van Winkle took place in 1922, but police departments had actually been employing women for many years before that. As early as 1845, New York City hired six women to work as jail matrons. Up until that time, men had taken care of all the duties involving both women prisoners and any women that came in contact with the police. This included searches, which, as might be imagined, led to many charges of sexual abuse. In 1873, Indiana estab-lished the first prison solely for women. Before that time, most locations had housed women prisoners in the same facilities as men, usually on different floors, but occasionally in cells next to each other. Conditions such as these led to the call by many reformers for police matrons.

These matrons, however, even though eventually hired all over the United States by the late 1800s, could not truly be considered police-women, as they didn't have any real police powers. They didn't carry weapons, couldn't make arrests, and so on. Consequently, in the early twentieth century, many groups began calling not just for the hiring of jail and prison matrons, but also for the hiring of women police officers.

The reason for this sudden desire for women police officers in the early 1900s is not well known: it came about because of the Suffrage Movement, but had nothing to do with giving women equal rights. Around the turn of the twentieth century, many members of the Suffrage Movement were upper-class women, proper ladies who suddenly found themselves being carted off to jail because of their illegal protests in favor of giving women the right to vote. At this time in our country's history, it was considered totally inappropriate for any man, other than a family member, to touch a lady. But then suddenly, because of the Suffrage Movement, upper-class women were being physically hauled away to jail by policemen. Most of these women were appalled not just over the fact that they were being manhandled by lower-class men, but also by the squalid condition of most of the jails the policemen took them to. Many people in society, besides wanting female officers to handle female prisoners, also felt that having women officers stationed at police facilities would force these locations to be cleaned up.

According to an article about the history of policewomen,

> The strong suffragette/feminist movement of the late 1890s and early 1900s caused a need for women on police forces. Male officers who had little interaction/dealings with "nice" (affluent) women in a work environment shocked the suffragettes' "sensibilities." These actions in turn led to more activism and repeated requests for female officers.[5]

Some women's organizations even used reverse psychology in an attempt to argue for women in policing. An 1890 magazine article about the New York City Police Department said,

> Mrs. Lowell, late Commissioner of Charities, has recently written to the Board of Police, referring to the appeal made to them by a body of most estimable women some months since to make the appointments, an appeal based upon the ground that common decency demanded that drunken and degraded women should be removed from the sight and hearing of the men and boys who are held at station houses.[6]

In addition to the violation of the suffragettes' sensibilities, another apparently common event also motivated the demand for the hiring of policewomen. An example was the conviction in June 1890 of a New York City police officer for the attempted rape of a fifteen-year-old girl held at a police station. Unfortunately, this was not an isolated incident. Women held at police stations often suffered sexual abuse. Reformers felt that if policewomen handled the cases of young girls brought to police stations, rather than policemen, then these types of incidents would stop.

Because of all these reasons, for many years the demand for women police officers came from groups such as the Suffrage Movement, the Women's Christian Temperance Union, the Federation of Women's Clubs, and many other civic groups. And also for many years, city administrators put off these demands, until finally one city gave in.

In 1908, Lola Baldwin, whose work for the Traveler's Aid Society at the 1905 Lewis and Clark Exposition in Portland, Oregon, involved ensuring that young women and juveniles stayed safe from aggressive men, so impressed city leaders that in 1908 the city of Portland appointed her as "Superintendent of the Women's Auxiliary to the Police Department for the Protection of Girls."[7] The chief presented her with a badge, Police Star No. 33. Baldwin served at the Portland Police Department for fourteen years. She proved so diligent in her job of closing brothels and other establishments of ill repute that she received several death threats and even reportedly received a package of poisoned tea. Interestingly, her office was not located at police headquarters, but rather at the local YWCA.

In 1910, Los Angeles followed suit and also hired a policewoman. Alice Stebbins Wells in 1909 had presented to the mayor a petition signed by many prominent citizens requesting the hiring of a policewoman in Los Angeles. Wells, a theology student and social worker, had for a number of years performed volunteer work with the youth of the city. However, she found that to be effective she had to go into some disreputable neighborhoods and establishments, usually by herself. Finally, she decided that she needed an escort into these neighborhoods and some authority to back up what she was trying to do. Being a police officer, she decided, would accomplish both of these goals. However, when she first inquired about this possibility, she met immediate rejection from the city fathers. And so she began gathering the signatures of prominent citizens. That did the trick. On September 12, 1910, after passage of a city ordinance allowing her appointment, the mayor of Los Angeles hired Wells as a police officer.

The chief of police, however, obviously didn't agree with the mayor's decision. According to an article in the March 1911 issue of *Good Housekeeping*, "In handing her the badge, the chief said he was sorry to offer a woman so plain an insignia of office; that when he had a squad of Amazons (Wells was only five feet tall) he would ask the police commission to design a star edged with lace ruffles."[8]

Regardless of the chief's opposition, the police department made Wells an officer and gave her, besides her badge, a rule book and a Gamewell key. (The Gamewell System was a collection of call boxes strategically located around a city. These boxes contained several levers that could be pulled, each lever sending a request to police headquarters for a different type of assistance.) In 1910 the idea of women police officers was still something totally novel in the United States. Officer Wells discovered this right away. In those days, streetcars allowed police officers to ride for free, but when Officer Wells showed her badge to the streetcar conductor he accused her of misusing her husband's badge and reported her. As a consequence, the chief of police gave her a badge that said "policewoman" on it. (Interestingly, we had a similar problem here in Indianapolis in the 1970s. The police department had instituted a take-home car program, and occasionally the department would receive complaints from citizens who saw a policewoman out of uniform driving her police car off duty. The citizens would complain that they'd seen a policeman's wife driving his police car.)

Procedures involving women that police officers came in contact with quickly changed at the Los Angeles Police Department. Following Alice Stebbins Wells' appointment, the chief of police issued an order that said, "No young girl can be questioned by a male officer. Such work is delegated solely to policewomen, who, by their womanly sympathy and intuition, are able to gain the confidence of their younger sisters."[9] As can be surmised by this order, the Los Angeles Police Department, following Officer Wells' appointment, soon began hiring more policewomen.

Regardless of stiff resistance by many city leaders across the United States, the pressure from women's groups and others to hire policewomen became so great that, two years after being appointed as a police officer, Alice Stebbins Wells took a six-month leave of absence from the Los Angeles Police Department to tour the country and talk to city administrators and others in positions of authority, trying to raise support for the hiring of policewomen. She delivered 136 lectures in seventy-three cities. "I have spoken all the way across the continent and

I shall speak all the way back," Officer Wells said in a 1912 *New York Times* article.[10]

Although Officer Wells received a mainly favorable response from most of the individuals and groups she spoke to, even inspiring some cities to begin hiring female officers, her reception wasn't always totally positive. When she attempted to address the International Association of Chiefs of Police Convention in Grand Rapids, Michigan, in 1914, she received an extremely hostile reception, nearly being thrown out of the meeting. "Call the patrol wagon!" one of the attendees shouted. "Another nut gone wrong!"[11]

During her career, Officer Wells, along with persuading the city of Los Angeles to hire her in 1910, also in 1915 helped found the International Association of Policewomen. Along with this, in 1918, she convinced the University of California to develop and offer a course for women in police work, and, in 1928, became the first president of the Women's Peace Officers Association of California.

Following the hiring of Officer Baldwin in 1908 and Officer Wells in 1910, other cities began hiring policewomen. In 1912, New York City hired the first woman police detective. Isabelle Goodwin, the widow of a police officer, had been doing undercover work for several years for the police department before her appointment as a detective. In 1914, San Francisco hired its first three policewomen, known as "The Three Kates," since they all coincidentally had the same first name.[12]

Los Angeles, after gaining recognition for hiring one of the first policewomen, also scored a first in 1916 when the city hired the first black policewoman, Georgia Robinson. Blacks, like women, had a long struggle before they could attain equality and respect within police departments.

Even though, as stated previously, many cities began adding women to their police forces because of pressure from civic and women's groups, early policewomen actually had very little to do with real police work. Most cities hired them as "social workers with badges," whose job it was to prevent crime by counseling misguided youth and young women going down the wrong path. Cities also hired them as "keepers of the community morals." Police departments assigned policewomen to visit and regulate dance halls, amusement parks, penny arcades, movie theaters, and other places where children and young women could get into trouble.

However, in the early twentieth century, whenever a new city administration took over, the program of policewomen was often abolished, although seldom for long. In Indianapolis, Indiana, for example, the city established the Indianapolis Police Department Women's Bureau in 1918. By 1921, the Bureau had grown to twenty-three policewomen, headed by Captain Clara Burnside. The success of the Indianapolis Police Department Women's Bureau garnered publicity from all over the world, and the city showcased it as the most efficient and effective Women's Bureau in the United States. However, by 1924 it had been disbanded. An incoming mayor did not approve of the idea of policewomen. Indianapolis would, of course, eventually rebound and begin hiring policewomen again.

Along with all the motives discussed so far, another reason behind the nationwide demand for the hiring of policewomen during the early twentieth century was the entry of the United States into World War I. Cities close to large military bases feared that the concentration of so many young men in the area would pose a threat to vulnerable young girls. And so, many groups pushed for cities to hire policewomen to protect these young girls.

A magazine article in December 1917 said,

Such is the glamour of the uniform. This glamour today is felt everywhere. It is causing flutters of emotion in thousands of feminine hearts ordinarily calm and impassive. . . . Each wearer is a possible hero. . . . One of the greatest needs of the city or town frequented by soldiers in their leisure hours is one or more sympathetic, experienced women with police powers to patrol the streets.[13]

World War I also broadened, at least for its duration, the duties of policewomen. An article in the *Boston Evening Transcript* of May 18, 1918, said of New York City policewomen, "It will be one of the duties of the policewomen to keep an eye on people who are believed to be spies, and to inform us what is going on. This will take some heavy work off the shoulders of the present force. They are going to keep a tab on people who incite to sedition."[14] Unfortunately, the end of the war also ended the expanded role policewomen played.

With the exception of the time during World War I, for the most part policewomen hired during the early twentieth century were not hired to perform any type of real police function, but rather to perform as social workers with badges. Interestingly, however, this is contrary to the drawings many newspapers featured whenever they printed articles about policewomen. Newspapers often included caricatures of tall, masculine, and mean-looking women, usually sporting a gun and wielding a large club.

These caricatures aside, most police administrators actually didn't give much thought to the idea of policewomen carrying guns or clubs. Most had a much more limited view of the duties of policewomen. Most police departments hired policewomen solely to handle cases involving women, girls, and very young boys. Their work was to be preventative rather than punitive. And as mentioned previously, a part of the job given to most policewomen was to be the protector of the community morals. To do this, police departments required them to regularly visit and monitor dance halls, movie theaters, amusement parks, penny arcades, skating rinks, and other places where immorality might thrive. The benefit of this to the police department, although seldom acknowledged, was that it relieved the policemen of this duty and allowed them to perform more challenging public safety jobs.

An article about Officer Alice Stebbins Wells in the March 1911 issue of *Good Housekeeping* said,

> She has found that there is scarcely a penny arcade whose pictures are not suggestive of evil. . . . Her duty in visiting picture shows is to see that no minors are admitted except in the company of a parent or legal guardian, and that no pictures are displayed at the entrance showing deeds of violent acts or questionable morality.[15]

In Los Angeles, policewomen's duties, along with those noted previously, also included "the suppression of unwholesome billboard displays, searches for missing persons, and the maintenance of a general information bureau for women seeking advice on matters within the scope of police departments."[16]

As is evident from these descriptions, even though women in the early twentieth century had finally made it onto police department rolls, they were still as yet far from being accepted as equals by the men of the department. Even August Vollmer, the chief of police of Berkeley, California, and one of the most revered historical crusaders for the modernization of police departments, had a very limited view of the role policewomen could play. In a March 1926 magazine article, he said, "Let us hasten the day when the policewoman shall be placed on the front line of police entrenchments in the battle against vice and crime as an active industrial, social, and child welfare worker."[17]

By 1930, he hadn't changed his opinion much when he said in another magazine article,

> My own opinion is that the right kind of woman does not need a uniform any more than other social workers do. . . . We note in passing that the lady cop is well-gowned as any of the women who have come from a morning's walk downtown, and that she holds her teacup as daintily as though her only contacts with the police department were by the way of the traffic signals on busy street corners.[18]

O. W. Wilson, a protégé of Vollmer who wrote what was considered until the late 1960s to be the bible of criminal justice studies, *Police Administration,* also held a very limited view of the value of policewomen. In *Police Administration* he stated that women were not the best choice to command units such as the Juvenile Branch because they are likely to become irritable and overly critical under stress, and that men made much better supervisors of women than other women did.[19]

Men, however, weren't the only ones who saw the role of policewomen as being minor compared with men's roles. Edith Abbott, a member of the International Association of Policewomen, said in a magazine article in April 1926,

> In the first place, in spite of the name "policewoman," the woman officer does not and should not do the kind of work our police officers are actually doing. She is not a "policeman" engaged primarily in detecting crime; she is a social worker engaged in the most difficult kind of public welfare work. . . . So the "policewoman" needs to be first of all these days a ma-

ture woman with the liberal education of a university and the professional education of a good school of social work.[20]

Indeed, supporting this viewpoint, many police departments in the early twentieth century required that their policewomen applicants have training and experience in social work.

Five years later, a 1931 statement by the International Association of Policewomen said, "The functions of the policewoman are primarily social—emphasis is on prevention of delinquency rather than apprehension and punishment of the offender."[21] Confirming this statement, a survey by a national magazine around this time found that in thirty-five out of forty cities surveyed, policewomen supervised dance halls. In thirty-four of the cities, policewomen also regularly patrolled movie theaters. In a smaller number of cities, according to the survey, policewomen also visited cabarets, skating rinks, and amusement parks, making more than 1,000 of these visits per year in Minneapolis, and 1,500 per year in Detroit.[22]

Finally, in 1936, Eleanor L. Hutzel, deputy commissioner of police for Detroit, said, "On the other hand, the work which women can do will always be minor as compared with what men can do."[23] Unfortunately, this attitude didn't change for many years. In January 1946, for example, the International Association of Chiefs of Police and the National Sheriff's Association published a manual titled *Techniques of Law Enforcement in the Use of Policewomen with Special Reference to Social Protection.*

Because of the limitations on their duties, most of these early policewomen didn't wear uniforms. In addition, most of these women, although issued a badge, also usually didn't carry a firearm because it was deemed unnecessary for the type of work they did. Victoria Murray, the director of policewomen for Detroit, said in 1921, "Our women do not know what guns are. They would not know what to do with them."[24]

It wasn't until the mid-1930s, over a quarter century after police departments began hiring the first female officers, that police departments finally began requiring policewomen to carry firearms and also to show proficiency with them at a target range. For example, in New York City in 1934, Police Commissioner Lewis J. Valentine was the first to institute the policy that the department's 155 policewomen carry a firearm of at least .32 caliber, and that, also for the first time, they report for target practice.

Even though policewomen's roles within most police departments were extremely limited, the men of the departments still often deeply resented this intrusion. And so, to pacify these men, most police departments with a substantial number of policewomen segregated the female officers into Women's Bureaus. These units, which were usually commanded by a woman and often housed separately from the rest of the police department (many times in a different building), typically involved themselves only in activities that involved women, girls, and occasionally very young boys.

According to one study on the history of policewomen, "Organized into separate women's bureaus, [policewomen] 'were removed from the male power base of the police organization, with a negative impact on the scope of their responsibilities, salaries, prestige, and opportunities for promotion.'"[25] Another source adds,

> As women sought more mainstream roles in policing, the arrangement of separate police bureaus became problematic. Many believed organization by gender limited the functions of the female officer and ghettoized the profession. Despite these concerns, most female officers accepted the women's bureaus as the only way to ensure that women remained in law enforcement. An additional problem involved hostility by male officers who wanted to disband women's bureaus. A particular point of contention was the fact that a woman usually oversaw the female divisions and many male officers felt that women should not be in leadership positions.[26]

Unfortunately, as I can attest to after thirty-eight years in law enforcement, this feeling has still not totally disappeared from police departments.

Amazingly, however, even though many police departments in the early twentieth century defined policewomen's roles as very limited, many of these police departments also made the requirements to be hired much higher for policewomen than for policemen. In 1922, at the 29th Annual Convention of the International Association of Chiefs of Police, a very influential law enforcement organization still active today, the membership endorsed the concept of policewomen. However, while attesting to the necessity of having policewomen, the association also put forth some very stringent requirements to become a policewoman. For example, members of the group felt that the minimum educational level for a policewoman should be graduation from a college or nursing school.[27]

As a consequence of this endorsement, many cities followed the association's recommendation and required high levels of education to become a policewoman. A study completed in 1929 concluded, "In no city are requirements for appointment as a woman officer lower than the requirements for appointment as a man officer, and in many cities the requirements for the women officers are very much higher."[28] As a comparison, in many police departments, a high school diploma for male officers didn't become mandatory until the late 1950s and early 1960s.

This high level of education required to become a policewoman naturally brought some very talented women into the law enforcement field. According to a March 1928 magazine article about policewomen recruits, "Policewomen, the tests applied seem to show, come from a higher intellectual stratum than the average run of policemen. They have better educational equipment and more often better technical training."[29]

In a 1944 article by Eleanor Hutzel, Deputy Police Commissioner of Detroit, she said of her policewomen, "Of the 22 officers appointed since 1940, all but two are college graduates, most of whom majored in sociology."[30] The educational level of the Detroit policemen was, of course, much lower.

Like World War I, America's entry in World War II saw a sharp reduction in the manpower available for police departments, and as a consequence many of these departments began hiring more women. An April 1943 article from Asheville, North Carolina, for example, told about that city using eight policewomen for traffic control. "If more policemen go into the army or war plants," the article said, "more women officers will be employed to handle the downtown intersections."[31] Still, however, as with World War I, following the end of World War II, policewomen returned to their gender-specific jobs within police departments, a situation that remained static until 1968.

As we discussed earlier in this chapter, persuading cities across the United States to hire policewomen took many years. In 1913, there were reportedly only thirteen female police officers in the United States. In 1925, 118 cities in the United States had hired policewomen, more than

200 cities by 1927, 290 cities by 1936, and by 1942 almost every city in the United States with a population more than 100,000 had policewomen on their force. In 1945, according to one count, police departments employed more than one thousand policewomen nationally. By 1950, the number of policewomen in our country had swelled considerably to a little over 2,600. By 1960, census figures showed that the number of policewomen in the United States had more than doubled in ten years and totaled 5,617. This, however, was still only a little over 2 percent of all the police officers nationally.

In this chapter we have talked exclusively about American police departments. However, many women in police departments in other countries faced similar problems. For example, in 1942, the Commissioner of Police in New Zealand had a strict rule that no policewomen could be married. The reason?

"When they marry they have to resign," said the Commissioner. "You see, we might want them for some job or other when they have to be home cooking their husband's dinner. That would not be much use to us, would it?"[32]

Last, while municipal police departments in the United States had been hiring policewomen from 1908 on, for almost fifty years after that most of these agencies did not allow policewomen to take part in promotional exams. Although a woman could become the commander of the Women's Bureau, that was usually the limit of the advancement policewomen could hope for. Only lawsuits by policewomen in the late 1950s and early 1960s finally forced police departments to allow policewomen to compete with the men for higher ranks within the department.

However, it wasn't only a difference in jobs, office location, salary, and promotional opportunities that separated policewomen from policemen during the early part of the twentieth century. Policewomen also suffered when it came to pensions, often receiving a reduced amount or no pension at all. An article in the *Journal of Criminal Law, Criminology, and Police Science,* talking about emergency policewomen appointed to the New York City Police Department during World War I, stated, "Their services proved so successful that by an act of the State Legislature in 1920 they were incorporated into the Police Department as Patrolwomen, *without pension benefits* [emphasis added]."[33] In Indianapolis, until a lawsuit in the 1970s changed it, the pension benefits for a retired policewoman expired when she died and her widower and any dependent children received nothing. The pension benefits for a deceased retired policeman, on the other hand, were transferred to his widow and any dependent children.

So far in this chapter we have talked totally about municipal police departments hiring policewomen. State police organizations and federal police agencies took many more years before they began hiring women as police officers. As a matter of fact, it wasn't until 1972 and the passage of civil rights legislation that the Secret Service and FBI finally began hiring female agents. It was also at about this same time that state police agencies began hiring their first female state troopers.

As can be seen, until 1968, policewomen played a very limited role in most police departments. The best they could hope for was a spot in the juvenile branch, a dispatcher position, or perhaps a clerical slot. After 1968, all of this changed and many women came into law enforcement with the intent of doing real police work. Liz and Betty opened the door for policewomen all over the world. But what makes women want to become police officers? Is it the same as what drives men to join? In the next chapter we look at the question of what motivates women to join police departments.

# 3

## MOTIVATIONS

"That's it. You're free to go," the paymaster at Travis Air Force Base told me.

In October 1968, I had finished my enlistment in the Air Force, where I spent my time during the Vietnam War working as an intelligence analyst. Since the last part of my enlistment had been at Hickam Air Force Base in Hawaii, my separation from the Air Force took place at Travis Air Force Base, located about fifty miles northeast of San Francisco.

At that time in my life, being just twenty-one years old, I had never given any thought at all to the idea of becoming a police officer. Instead, I had, from my earliest memories, wanted to be a writer. Consequently, rather than returning to Indianapolis, where I had grown up, I thought that San Francisco, with its free-thinking atmosphere, would be the perfect place for a writer to get started. And so I found a small apartment and started getting settled in. Interesting and turbulent times rumbled through San Francisco in the late 1960s, and I felt certain they would inspire my writing career to take off soon.

Unfortunately, in December 1968, my stepmother was diagnosed with cervical cancer, the same type of cancer that had killed my mother nine years before. My father, naturally upset by this discovery, called me in California and asked me to come home for a bit. My stepmother is a wonderful woman who has always given her stepchildren as much love as she does her birth children. So, I immediately went to see my landlord and paid my apartment rental for a month ahead, certain I would return by then. Following this, I went to the airport and caught a flight to Indianapolis.

As it turned out, my visit to Indianapolis proved to be more expensive and last longer than I had thought it would. Consequently, I soon found myself running low on funds. I didn't want to borrow money that I had no idea when I could pay back, so I began looking around for a job that would give me enough cash to get back to California. Unfortunately, most of the short-term jobs I looked into didn't pay much at all.

My brother, Fred, had joined the Indianapolis Police Department the year before, and, seeing I wasn't having much luck raising money, told me that the police department was hiring. He explained that the first five months at the department would be mostly classroom instruction at the training academy, and that it should be pretty easy for me since I had always been an excellent student.

"Try it for a few months," Fred told me. "If you don't like it you can quit, and you'll still have enough money to get back to California."

I checked and found that the salary for recruits at the Indianapolis Police Department looked much better, actually paying almost twice as much as any of the other jobs I had looked into. Also, I reasoned, the experience I would get at the police department training academy would probably be very valuable later as a writer. And so, I went down to the police department to put in an application. The lieutenant in charge of recruiting there welcomed me into his office, and not only took my application, but also had me take the police department entrance exam the same day.

In those days, I found, while the Vietnam War still raged on, police departments all across the United States were having a very difficult time finding qualified candidates. Since I was an honorably discharged veteran with a top-secret clearance, and, according to the lady grading my exam, had just made excellent scores on the police department entrance test, the lieutenant in charge of recruiting set me up for interviews the next week, and a background investigation the following week. As a result, two weeks after applying I had been accepted for the next Indianapolis Police Department recruit class. And so, still expecting to stay there for only a few months, I joined thirty-nine other police officer trainees in the February 1969 class.

At the training academy, during breaks and at lunch, the other recruits often talked about themselves and their motivations for joining the Indianapolis Police Department. We had ten policewomen in our recruit class, and after listening to them I found that they had a number of different reasons for joining the police department. One woman, who sat directly behind me, had wanted to be a police officer since she was a little girl. It was all she had ever dreamed of being. And since Indianapolis, in 1969, had become the most progressive police department in the United States for policewomen, she had joined with the intention of following in the path Liz and Betty had carved out. She told me that she wanted a job with excitement and challenge, and that police work was all she had ever considered.

I soon discovered that the father of one of the policewomen who sat a few rows in front of me was a lieutenant at that time on the Indianapolis Police Department. Consequently, she had grown up hearing almost every day about police work, and had decided to continue the family tradition, something I later found to be prevalent in the Indianapolis Police Department; often four or five members of a family served in the department. At one time, four members of my own family served on the Indianapolis Police Department. Later on during my career, I discovered that this clustering of family members on police departments was by no means restricted to the Indianapolis Police Department, but was something widespread in police departments everywhere.

In addition to the policewoman with a father in the department, I also discovered that two of the other policewomen in my recruit class had husbands who were police officers. Police officers being married to other officers was again something I found to be very common in police departments.

Another policewoman in my class did not have any relatives in the department, but instead talked a lot about her desire to do something for the community. She told me that she wanted a job that would allow her to have a positive impact on other people's lives. She wanted a job that would allow her to accomplish something worthwhile. She wanted to make a difference.

About half the policewomen, however, didn't have such lofty goals, but instead had joined because the pay and benefits at the Indianapolis Police Department proved to be much better than they could get anywhere else on only a high school education. For many years, policewomen at the Indianapolis Police Department, even though serving in only minor law enforcement roles, had nevertheless received the same pay and benefits as policemen. In addition, the Indianapolis Police Department, founded in 1854, had never had a layoff (and still hasn't). As a matter of fact, I served as commander of the Personnel Branch at the Indianapolis Police Department for six years, and, although there were police department layoffs in the states all around us, I faced the opposite problem of never being able to hire enough police officers to keep our strength up to budgeted numbers; I almost always needed another fifty or sixty officers. As a result, for a woman—or a man, for that matter—the Indianapolis Police Department provided a secure and well-paying job with great benefits.

≋

After my recruit training, I naturally met hundreds of other policewomen during my career at the Indianapolis Police Department, including the woman I eventually married. What were the reasons for these women wanting to become police officers?

Melanie, who joined the Indianapolis Police Department as a civilian worker in 1977 and became a sworn police officer just a few weeks after we married in 1980, joined for the same reason as many policewomen: She had been a divorced woman with two children, and she saw this as a great opportunity for financial security.

"The job offered me security, good pay, good benefits, and I could provide for my family," she told me. "I had originally planned on joining the military after high school, but I ended up getting married instead. The Indianapolis Police Department turned out to be a real blessing for me."[1]

As an interesting side note, in 1968, when my future wife was still a teenager, Liz Coffal and Betty Blankenship, the first two policewomen on street patrol, arrived at her house to take a stolen car report. Both Melanie and her younger sister, impressed by how sharp the two policewomen looked, bombarded them with questions about becoming a policewoman. My wife's sister was particularly interested, and decided right then that she would become a policewoman when she grew up. However, it was my wife who instead became an officer, whereas her sister enlisted in the Army and became a nurse.

Interestingly, a very similar thing happened to Liz Coffal, one of the policewomen who had so impressed my wife. "When I was a teenager, I met Indianapolis policewoman Cloe Clark," Liz told me. "She looked so sharp in her uniform, and she acted so professional that I thought right then that this was what I wanted to do. Right then I knew that I wanted to be just like her and spend the rest of my life helping people.

"However," Liz went on, "when I first applied at the Indianapolis Police Department they said they weren't hiring policewomen right then, and I found out later that they hadn't hired any for over four years. But I didn't give up, and when I went back a couple years later they hired me. I eventually ended up being Cloe's partner for awhile."[2]

According to Betty Blankenship's daughter, Robin Tryon, Betty's life's dream had first been to join the Navy. "But Mom got married right out of high school and had children. So she began looking around and decided that joining the police department, with its paramilitary structure, would be close to her dream of the Navy. She applied in 1964, but got turned down because they weren't hiring any policewomen then.

"Mom finally got hired in 1967, just before she reached the mandatory age of thirty-three. She was elated. She wanted to be a real police officer. It didn't occur to her when the police department hired her that she wouldn't have the same opportunities as policemen. So she was really disappointed when she found out. But she and Liz were able to overcome that obstacle."[3]

Like several of the policewomen in my class, Betty also had a family member join the department. In 1990, her daughter, Robin Tryon, joined the Indianapolis Police Department. Naturally, Betty had served as a role model for Robin.

"What she has done," Robin said of her mother in 1990, "without realizing it, has been phenomenal for women in law enforcement."[4] In an interview five years later, Robin added, "She [Betty Blankenship] had to put up with criticism. I was able to step into the job and do the work without justifying myself."[5]

However, when Robin told her mother that she wanted to follow in her footsteps and also join the police department, Robin didn't get the reaction she had expected. "Mom wasn't happy," Robin told me. "The dynamics of the police department had changed dramatically from 1967 to 1990, becoming more of a business than a family. Also, she worried because being on the street was more dangerous in 1990 than it had been in 1967. But when I graduated from the Training Academy Mom was really proud. It was really great to have a Mom who was a police officer because I had someone I could talk to about things that happened in the police department, and she'd understand what I was talking about."[6]

I asked Robin if her mother had given her any advice when she joined the police department. "She told me to keep my gun hand free," Robin said. "Always keep my gun hand free. It was kind of odd advice for a mother to give to a daughter, but that's how it is in a police family."[7]

The information I've provided so far in this chapter applies exclusively to the Indianapolis Police Department. Do the same motivations drive women to sign up at other police departments across the United States?

Ella Bully-Cummings, appointed as the chief of police of Detroit in 2003, had an experience very similar to Liz's and my wife's. Working as a ticket cashier in a Detroit movie theater in the mid-1970s, she encountered a policewoman in uniform. The aura of confidence and professionalism that the policewoman radiated impressed Bully-Cummings so much that several years later she joined the Detroit Police Department.

I asked a female chief of police in Minnesota what made her want to join. "I grew up in a small town, on a farm, and always enjoyed the outdoors," Carol Sletner, chief of the Roseville, Minnesota, Police Department, told me. "In the eighth grade, I took a career interest test and the results pointed me in the direction of law enforcement. I really liked the idea of being outside, of never knowing what is going to happen from day to day, and of getting to meet new people. To this day, I can't think of a better job to have."[8]

Of course, like three of the policewomen in my recruit class, a large number of policewomen across the country applied at police departments because they had been exposed to police work through family members who are police officers. For instance, Robin Estrada joined the Milwaukee Police Department because her uncle and father were police officers.

"He was my sergeant and he was my lieutenant," Robin said of her uncle. "He didn't treat me any different than anyone else."[9]

The small town of Malverne, New York, in July 2007 swore in its first female police officer, Joanne McNelis. "I'm just very honored," McNelis said upon taking the oath of office to become a police officer. "I grew up here, and to be a part of the community in a way that I thought would never happen—I felt like a little kid on Christmas morning."[10] Both McNelis's father and husband are police officers.

A number of policewomen across the country don't have family members who are police officers, but instead have worked in fields close to law enforcement and have consequently found themselves attracted to the work. For example, Elizabeth Granados of Santa Ana, California, attended the University of California at Irvine. While there, she interned in the media relations unit of the Santa Ana Police Department. Being there and working closely with law enforcement drew her into the profession.

"I've always been interested in the law enforcement side, but being an intern I realized there was so much more to police work than just giving tickets," Granados said. "I knew I wanted a rewarding career and to be able to give back to the community because, ultimately, I'm part of that community."

In April 2008, Granados, though only five feet and three inches tall, graduated number one out of thirty-eight recruits at the Orange County Sheriff's Training Academy. "To see her come out No. 1 was a thrill for the department, because it's such a competitive and highly stressful environment," said Paul Walters, chief of police of the Santa Ana Police Department, where Granados became a member.[11]

Although I may at one time have thought that my own experience and reasons for joining the Indianapolis Police Department were unique, I've found them to be quite the opposite. Take retired Chief Karin Montejo of the Miami-Dade Police Department who now runs Montejo Consulting, Inc., for example. She told me:

In 1976, I graduated from the University of Florida. My father died the day after I graduated, so I came home to take care of things, and soon found I needed a job. I heard the Miami-Dade Police Department was hiring dispatchers, so I interviewed for a dispatcher position. During the interview, the sergeant conducting it said, "Hang on a second." Then he played the tape of a man calling 911. The man had called the police and said, "She's going to kill me." Then you heard him being stabbed.

The sergeant said to me, "Do you want to take that call as a dispatcher, or do you want to go out and find out who did that?" He actually pointed me toward the police academy, and so I joined.[12]

Some policewomen, however, were so impressed by what Liz and Betty accomplished at the Indianapolis Police Department that they entered law enforcement because they wanted to be a part of the movement of women into previously male-only police jobs. For example, in 1974 a job announcement for the California Highway Patrol (CHP) had the words "FOR MEN ONLY" stamped across it. Protests from women finally brought about a lawsuit that the California State Legislature quickly resolved by requiring CHP to conduct a two-year study on the feasibility of having women on their department. In October 2002, one of the first women hired under this study retired from CHP.

In another case, Donna Ash Brown, the first female officer in the Putnam, Connecticut, Police Department, said, "When I was a little girl growing up here, I always said I wanted to be an officer but was told girls couldn't be policemen."[13] Like Liz and Betty, she joined the police department and proved them wrong.

"I put my application in and there were no females and I wanted to accomplish something that hadn't been accomplished, and I did that," said police sergeant Deborah Devane, the first policewoman to be hired by the Dothan, Alabama, Police Department.[14]

Officer Michele Brandt of the Omaha, Nebraska, Police Department told me:

When I was in the third grade, a male police officer came to our class. I remember asking him how many women police officers Omaha had. The officer laughed at me, saying, "Women can't be police officers. Next question."

I felt so humiliated for even asking. As I grew up, I continued to ask every police officer I saw, and pretty much got the same response. In high school, I joined the Explorers Program, but they wouldn't let me sign up for law enforcement; I could only sign up for "girl" things.

As soon as possible I applied to be an Omaha police officer. I was hired on my first try, and have not regretted a day since. Now, every time I hear young people, especially young ladies, express a desire to be a police officer, I tell them to try for the career they want, and not to listen to anyone else.[15]

In addition to the many reasons given so far, many women, like the policewomen in my recruit class, became police officers because they wanted to do something important; they wanted to do something to make the community a better place to live. These women were looking for a career that they knew would mean something and make a difference in the world. A good example of this is Jacquelyn H. Barrett.

In November 1992, Barrett became the Fulton County, Georgia, sheriff, something unheard of for a black woman in the south. Looking back at what motivated her to enter law enforcement more than twenty years before the election that made her sheriff, she talked about growing up during the Civil Rights Movement and not liking how the police responded to protesters. "I didn't like [what I saw] but I could still take a step back and say, 'This is incredible. I think I'd like to do something with that, to change that. But I'd prefer to do it from the inside, rather than fight for change from the outside.'"[16]

I also found that many policewomen, like Chief Sletner discussed previously, say that they came to law enforcement because they wanted a job that offered variety, excitement, and didn't involve sitting behind a desk or standing behind a counter all day. "I was attracted by the excitement of different types of people and situations," a policewoman told a researcher who asked her about her reasons for wanting to become a police officer.[17]

For the most part, I found that women enter law enforcement for the same reasons as men. Also, like men, most of the women, once they have worked for a short time as police officers, find that they simply can't let go, that this is the job they want to make a career of and spend the rest of their lives doing.

In my own case, which I discussed at the beginning of this chapter, although I had only intended on staying at the Indianapolis Police

Department for a few months in order to earn enough money to get back to California, once I went out on patrol as a part of our recruit training I was hooked. I stayed at the Indianapolis Police Department for thirty-eight years, holding such positions as street captain, captain of detectives, police department executive officer, and commander of the homicide branch. It was a decision I've never regretted because not only did I find a tremendously fulfilling career that I loved, but the job also helped propel my writing career by giving me tons of material to use.

Throughout this chapter we have talked about the many reasons women joined police departments following Liz and Betty's smashing of the street patrol barrier in Car 47. As we will see in the next chapter, being Car 47 didn't, at first at least, measure up to all that Liz and Betty had hoped it would. Instead, the two pioneering policewomen found that not only did they face stiff opposition, but that before they would be allowed to do any real police work they first had to prove themselves to the men.

# 4

## CAR 47

**"T**he night before Betty and I went out in Car 47, it was so exciting," Liz told me. "At last, we had our chance to show that women could do the job of street patrol. But Betty and I also knew that we couldn't screw this up because it would set women back years.

"I got chills when I first got into the police car," Liz added. "I told myself, 'This is real. This is really going to happen.' For the first hour Betty and I both kept saying, 'We can't believe we're doing this. We can't believe we're really doing this.'" But then, after the initial elation, reality set in very quickly.

"We really thought that as Car 47 we were going to be able to go out and tear the hell out of the city's criminals," Liz said. "But as it turned out, for the first couple of months we didn't do any real police work at all."[1]

As Liz said, the first couple of months didn't turn out at all as she and Betty had envisioned. Ever since recruit class the two women had dreamed of being patrol officers, of being sent on the same type of runs that the policemen received, of being able to show that a woman could do the job of patrol as well as a man. But it didn't turn out to be quite that way. Instead, for the first couple of months the dispatchers gave Liz and Betty every tedious run that the male officers didn't want to take, the type of runs that were mostly a lot of report writing, waiting for ambulances, and wasted time.

On their first day, for example, along with doing press interviews and posing for publicity photos, the two policewomen answered the call of a woman having a stroke and another call of a woman going into labor. They summoned ambulances for both, and that was the most excitement they got. In the following days, Liz and Betty continued to be sent on runs that the male officers didn't want to take. According to Liz's police department notebook, on the second day they received three radio runs: a hemorrhaging woman, an unconscious man, and a stolen vehicle report. The following day involved one sick woman run, and that was it.

Reading through one of Car 47's early monthly run logs, I found that Liz and Betty received for one month two motor verifications, which involved checking a vehicle's identification number for a new car title; two stolen vehicle verifications; eighteen report runs that involved larcenies, vandalisms, trouble with children, trash dumped in an alley, and a man exposing himself; twelve abandoned car reports; two juvenile prisoner transports; two lost children reports; one death notification; three runs to search female prisoners; one property damage accident report; three animal bite reports; four residence burglary reports; one missing elderly person report; six parking violations; three heart attacks; and a half dozen DOAs (dead on arrival). There was not a single run in this bunch that involved any excitement at all. But what really dashed Liz and Betty's dream of doing real street patrol work was that, in addition to receiving just these mundane runs, at first Car 47 was only allowed to work during daylight hours.

While all of this was a huge disappointment to the two policewomen, it really shouldn't have been such a surprise. The press releases from the Indianapolis Police Department about Liz and Betty's new assignment in Car 47 had said that the two women would be assigned "service runs" in order to free up policemen for more important law enforcement duties. While this certainly wasn't what Liz and Betty had envisioned when they first discussed with Chief Churchill their desire to go out on street patrol, Churchill was much too politically astute to allow them free rein at first. He knew that the public and other police officers would not accept an immediate use of policewomen for all types of police runs. The program had to be implemented in carefully planned stages, and this would be just the first one.

An article about Liz and Betty in the September 11, 1968, issue of the *Indianapolis Star* said, "'Their performance will be observed closely,' said Chief Winston L. Churchill, 'both in Indianapolis and by other big departments around the country to determine whether more police-women should be assigned to service calls, freeing the men to concentrate more on crime.'"[2]

However, an article in the *Indianapolis News* on September 16, 1968, seemingly able to see into the future, said, "It seems improbable that we will soon see a policewoman apprehend stick-up men or shoot it out with criminals. But then again it seemed unlikely, not too long ago, that we would see them driving patrol cars."[3]

It quickly became clear to Liz and Betty that, despite their dreams in the training academy, they hadn't been put out onto the street as equals to the men, but rather to act in a secondary, support role by taking the minor runs and leaving the more exciting and dangerous ones to the men. Even their uniforms said they weren't equal. The chief insisted that they wear blouses, skirts, and high heels; and while certainly ladylike, this was hardly the uniform for someone who might get into a foot-chase or a fight. (This wouldn't change until December 1969 when Chief Churchill authorized calf-high boots in the place of high heels, and in March 1971 when he would authorize a pantsuit for policewomen.) Liz and Betty weren't even allowed to wear their guns on a belt as the men did. Instead, they had to keep them hidden in their purses at all times. This, of course, created some problems in that Liz and Betty always had to keep their purses close to them.

"The first uniform was terrible," Liz said. "You just couldn't do what you needed to do in a skirt and high heels and carrying a heavy purse. One time, I had my purse over my shoulder and when I leaned down to help a lady it swung around and hit her in the mouth."[4]

An article in *Indianapolis Magazine* said, "Since he had stuck his administrative neck out in the first place, Churchill told the two not to carry holsters. . . . [H]e didn't want it to look as though the two were looking for trouble."[5]

Despite this requirement to keep their guns hidden, an article in the September 13, 1968, issue of the *Indianapolis News* began with the statement, "*Pistol packin'* policewomen Miss Elizabeth Coffal and Mrs. Betty Blankenship manned a squad car yesterday to the amazement of citizens, the chagrin of some colleagues, and to the delight of themselves [emphasis added]."[6]

Liz, however, told me an interesting story about what happened the first time they did have to pull their guns out of their purses:

> We had a run to assist a policeman with a female runaway who'd been caught with an older man. When the man found out that he was going to jail, he tried to grab the policeman's gun, and a struggle started. Betty and I both pulled out our revolvers, but the officer was able to get control of the man and handcuff him. As it turned out, about the time we had our guns out a sergeant pulled up, and he was just aghast at the fact that policewomen had actually pulled their guns out on a man.
>
> So he takes us right into the Deputy Chief's Office and tells the chief what he saw. The deputy chief turned to us and asked what we had planned to do. Betty and I both told him that if the guy had gotten control of the policeman's gun we were going to shoot him. The deputy chief nodded and said, "All right, keep up the good work." And that was it.[7]

Soon afterward, because Liz and Betty were so upset about the safety issue, to say nothing of the inconvenience, of having to carry their revolvers in their purses, Chief Churchill told them to try to come up with a more functional, but still ladylike, uniform that would solve the problem. "We came up with what looked like a maternity top," Liz said. "We could wear our guns out of sight underneath it, and do away with having to carry them in our purses."[8]

Interestingly enough, however, even though Liz and Betty weren't supposed to display their revolvers, except in dire emergencies, Liz was an expert shot, much better than most of the men on the police department. In June 1968, Liz and three other policewomen won the National Police Pistol Championship, and in the same year Liz won the Indiana State Pistol Championship. She did all of this despite the fact she had never fired a revolver until she came on the police department.

So for the first couple of months of being Car 47, with the exception of the one minor scuffle during which they had to pull out their revolvers, Liz and Betty hadn't had any excitement at all. Instead, they had taken dozens of stolen-vehicle reports, sick-person runs, DOAs, vandalism reports, and trouble-with-children runs. "You would just be amazed at how many people die in a city this size, because we got every one of them," Betty told *The Indiana Trooper* magazine. "I don't know how many there were, but it seems to me that's all we got."[9] (According to one report, Car 47 received fourteen DOA runs in a two-week period; several of the bodies were three or four days old.[10]) And so, at the end of several months on the street, not only had Liz and Betty not received a single really juicy run, but they both also realized that the dispatchers weren't going to give them any. Consequently, they decided they were going to have to do something about it themselves.

"We want desperately to show these men that we are capable," Betty told a reporter, "that we don't lose our heads and we can function efficiently in an emergency."[11]

And so, to change their status of only taking service runs, Liz and Betty began listening closely to the police radio, and whenever a hot run came out anywhere close to them they sped toward it. They began going in on domestic disturbances, bar fights, robberies in progress, and other runs that most policemen thought women couldn't handle. The two women knew that they were taking a huge chance. One screw-up and Car 47 would be history.

Both women also knew that most of the policemen on the street resented their intrusion, particularly on hot runs, and so Liz and Betty made it a point to never appear to be overbearing or act as though they already knew it all. Actually, they knew very little. At this time, most of the patrol cars in Indianapolis were one-officer cars. But still, new policemen, before they were sent out on solo patrol, usually rode with a senior officer for several months and received on-the-job training. Liz and Betty received no such training.

"We were put out on the street with no training whatever," Liz said. "We had to monitor both radio frequencies, but we had no idea how to even answer the radio. We also didn't know what the radio codes meant. At first, whenever we'd get a run, we'd both look at each other and say, 'What'd he say?' We weren't very street savvy at all."[12]

An article in *Indianapolis Magazine* talked about Liz and Betty's lack of training, "They brushed up on first aid and drove to a fire station to find out how to use a resuscitator which they happened to find in the trunk after more than a week on the job. (Every police car is provided with one.) They even had to learn radio codes on their own and how to use the police log book."[13] Betty added to this, "They called us off vacation and put us out the next day. We didn't know anything when we started out—forms were one of our biggest problems."[14]

Also, in an attempt to make themselves appear less threatening to the male officers, Liz and Betty would always ask for advice from the policemen at the various runs they went in on, whether they already knew the answer or not. They hoped this would make the policemen feel superior, and perhaps a little less antagonistic toward them.

"Sometimes, we'd call for the men to explain something, even though we knew how to do it, just to give them a chance to show their experience," Liz said.[15]

But sometimes they didn't already know the answer, and so Betty added, "We decided from the beginning that if we didn't know how to do something we weren't just going to go ahead because we'd get criticized more for doing it wrong than we would for asking."[16]

Along with going in on hot runs, Liz and Betty, because they so desperately wanted the Car 47 program to continue, took every dull assignment the dispatchers gave them without argument. They also made a pact to never complain no matter how badly they were treated by the other police officers. They felt that this was the only way they could get the men to respect them. But they also had a plan for how they were going to change things in addition to going in on nearby hot runs. The two policewomen, in the empty time between radio runs, began initiating their own investigations by checking businesses and stopping suspicious vehicles and individuals. On one run, which involved a woman who had been beaten to death, Liz and Betty arrested her murderer, without the assistance of any policemen. Soon, the two women began to successfully handle more and more dangerous runs, both initiated by them and the ones close to them that they heard on the police radio.

Liz and Betty, however, also understood very clearly that many of the policemen in the department and, for that matter, all across the country, were watching for any slip-up that would prove, at least to them, that policewomen shouldn't be on the street. Policemen and police administrators all across the country were waiting for that one serious mistake that they could grab onto and use to demand that Chief Churchill cancel his program and put things back to the way they had

always been, with policewomen in a subordinate role at police headquarters, not on the street.

This worried the two women so badly that in a personal letter to Liz,
who was on vacation, Betty wrote about how she had run out of gasoline
while on patrol. She told Liz that she had called a friend at headquarters,
swore him to secrecy, and then had him bring gasoline out to her car.[17]
Interestingly, however, while this worried Betty, running out of gasoline
like this was not an unheard of problem for policemen, who, meaning to
get the gas tank filled up, would instead keep getting one hot run after
another until the gas tank was empty. A city wrecker would then bring
the gasoline out to them. It happened to me and other policemen. But
Betty knew that everyone would jump on this as a foul-up by a woman.

Also, because Liz and Betty knew that policemen and police administrators everywhere were watching them, they took extreme care, even
though they were taking on more and more dangerous runs, to never do
anything that would get them or someone else hurt, which they knew
would only give these policemen and police administrators ammunition.
They took extreme care not to give these individuals anything that they
could flaunt as proof that policewomen shouldn't be on the street. This
worry so haunted Liz and Betty that once when Betty injured herself
turning over a refrigerator that had been dumped in an alley with the
door still attached, she didn't make an official report as required by police department policy. To keep the matter secret, rather than going to
the police surgeon, she went to her own private doctor for help.

Liz also told me, "One time I slipped on the ice and really busted
my rear. I really thought I had broken something. But I didn't tell anyone because I knew some of the guys would say, 'See, they shouldn't
be out here.'"[18]

And yet, while Liz and Betty felt certain that any serious injury would
be used against them, policemen regularly suffer injuries as a part of
their job. During my first five years on the street, for example, I received
a serious slice wound to my hand, severe claw and teeth injuries to my
arm, a swollen eye from being punched, and a broken nose. However,
no one stood up and loudly exclaimed that this showed me to be unfit.
Rather, other policemen saw it as typical and simply part of the job.

Betty told *The Indiana Trooper* magazine, "Liz and I made an agree-
ment that when we went out in the car, we weren't out there for personal

glory. We were there to make that car work, so that somebody else could come out after us." She then added, "If we got hurt, we went and took care of it on our own, paid for it ourselves. We never told a soul, not once."[19] She told another publication, "We have a big responsibility and if this program doesn't work out we feel it will be our fault."[20]

After several months, their plan to initiate their own runs or simply go in on hot runs close by finally began to pay dividends. In March 1969, Liz and Betty made a self-initiated arrest for statutory rape. In March and April 1969, they also made several arrests in self-initiated drug investigations. In October 1969, they single-handedly arrested an escapee from the Kankakee, Illinois, Institution for the Criminally Insane. The man, when Liz and Betty encountered him, had blood all over him. They later found out that he had severely beaten a man who had made the mistake of picking up a hitchhiker. In addition, in October 1969, the two policewomen arrested five burglars.

But while all of this self-initiated activity helped them gain acceptance as real police officers, Liz and Betty also knew that, in order for the policemen to truly accept them as equals, they had to first prove themselves as being tough in a fight. Liz told me about one run that helped them do this:

> One day on Car 47 we heard a couple of cars get a run to arrest a woman on a warrant. We got there first, but when we did we found that the woman had a baby in her arms and she told us that if we came near her she'd throw the baby. When we very carefully approached her, sure enough she threw the little girl. Luckily, I was pretty quick and caught the baby.
>
> This was a pretty good-sized woman, and when she found out that the threat to throw the baby wasn't going to work she started fighting us. She put up a pretty good fight, but we finally got her in handcuffs. The man who had called the police about the woman watched the whole fight, and he just went on and on to the news media and to the other police officers that showed up about how tough Betty and I were. That helped quite a bit to impress the guys, and to show them that we could hold our own.[21]

As Liz and Betty began to successfully handle more and more dangerous and complex runs, more and more of the policemen on the department began to grudgingly admit that perhaps some women could do the job after all. Even the dispatchers, who at first would not give Liz and Betty anything but the easiest and safest runs, eventually began to see that these two women could handle almost anything, and began to assign them regular runs like the ones given to the policemen.

However, this was both good and bad for Liz and Betty. One time a dispatcher sent them on what turned out to be a phony run at what appeared to be a dope house. Liz and Betty asked who had called the police, and everyone at the address denied calling. Both women later said that they sensed something very wrong and evil there, and so they backed out carefully. Later, an investigation found out that the narcotics traffickers at the dope house had called in the phony police run with the intention of killing the policemen who answered it. But when the traffickers saw it was policewomen answering the call they apparently changed their minds. Liz and Betty both realized how close they had come to being killed, but at the same time felt good because they knew they had likely saved several police officers' lives.

Through all of their efforts, Liz and Betty finally began seeing evidence that little by little they were winning over many of the policemen to the idea of policewomen on the street. And while some policemen would never be won over, after enough time a majority finally did begin to see a place for women on street patrol. Consequently, there wasn't nearly the outcry there had been about Car 47 when Chief Churchill began expanding the program and assigning more women to street patrol.

"Betty and I decided that to really make the program work, we needed another team of policewomen to cover when we were on days off, on vacation, or were sick," Liz told me. "So we went and asked the chief about it, and he finally agreed."[22] About two years after Car 47 first went out, other policewomen also began being assigned to street patrol in Indianapolis. Liz said,

> When we went out, it wasn't to set a record or to set the world on fire, or even to be the first. We just wanted to do police work. We wanted to pave the way so that any policewomen who wanted to do this could. Before we went out, all the policewomen had desk jobs or worked with juveniles. And while this has its merits, Betty and I just wanted to do police work. And we did.[23]

In one of the interviews I had with Liz, I asked her if in September 1968 she realized that she and Betty were making history. "No," she told me, "we didn't realize it at the time, though of course it occurred to us later. Betty and I just wanted to be cops. We just wanted to have the same opportunities the men had."[24]

I asked Betty's daughter, Robin, the same question about her mother. "No," Robin told me, "Mom just wanted to be the police. She wanted to do the job and help people. It didn't occur to her at the time that this was something policewomen in other cities didn't do."[25]

In 1968, Liz and Betty took a daring step, and through their perseverance and hard work made police administrators all across the country see that the world wouldn't suddenly collapse and revert to barbarism if they put policewomen on street patrol. Actually, some police administrators, although opposed to the idea at first, realized that perhaps the program's success could turn out to be a good thing for them after all. They realized that, using policewomen, they would be able to supplement their numbers on street patrol, while at the same time solving certain problems they had been faced with for many years. Putting policewomen on the street would mean that they would now have women available immediately for the searches of female prisoners, to speak on the scene with sexual assault victims, for runs involving young children who the policemen might frighten, and for many other tasks.

Consequently, as we will see in the next chapter, following the success of Car 47 in Indianapolis, policewomen all across the country, although at first in small numbers, began appearing on street patrol and in many other previously male-only police positions. Like Car 47, however, this often wasn't a smooth transition, but rather a move vigorously opposed by the majority of the men on these police departments and often by the public at large.

**5**

# REACTION TO THE
# ADVANCEMENT OF POLICEWOMEN

"Car 47, check the security of a building, 2540 North College," the police radio blared.

My partner and I were cruising in our police car north on Rural Street, waiting for our next run. Since the run the dispatcher had just given out wasn't our car number or even terribly close to our patrol beat, I didn't give the radio call much concern.

"Goddammit!" my partner exclaimed as he slammed his hand against the steering wheel. "Come on, we'd better go over there and cover their asses or they'll get themselves in trouble."

"Why?" I asked. "What's wrong?"

Car 47 seemed to have been given a typical radio run that didn't require any extra help. This address, I knew, had a faulty burglar alarm system that sent in at least one false alarm every day. My partner's concern, however, made me think that maybe I, being a brand new officer, had missed something important I shouldn't have.

My partner, an officer with twenty-five years on the department, gave me the look of a parent dealing with a particularly slow child. "It's the pussy patrol," he said, making a U-turn on Rural Street and then turning right and heading west on 25th Street.

"Pussy patrol?" I asked, not knowing what he was talking about.

I had been out of the recruit class at the Indianapolis Police Department now for a little less than a month. As was tradition at the department, new recruits rode with older, experienced officers for six months
or so before they were allowed to patrol solo. Unfortunately, in 1969 the
program wasn't well planned or coordinated, and consequently the police department didn't have any older officers specifically selected and
trained to act as field training officers. The captain simply put a new officer with whoever was available. And while I rode with some excellent
officers, who taught me many important things about police work, I also
worked with some officers who, giving them the absolute best benefit of
the doubt, should have been fired. The one I rode with this day sat on
the borderline between these two groups.

"You know," he answered to my inquiry, "those policewomen
Churchill put out here. Jesus, what an idiot! Women don't belong out
in police cars. I don't give a damn what anybody says, it's never going
to work."

My partner then began jabbing his finger in my direction like a sword
thrust. "But I'll tell you what's going to happen. All the chief's going to
do with his brilliant idea is get somebody hurt or killed. I don't care what
anybody says, women don't belong out in police cars. I tell you, they're
going to get themselves or some poor policeman hurt real bad. That
Churchill, what a dumbass!"

I knew about the policewomen in Car 47, of course, but hadn't as yet
encountered them in my short career. Since they were the only female
patrol officers in the city at that time, the chances of running into them
were pretty slim.

"You wait and see," my partner went on, "the chief is going to wish he
hadn't done this. He's going to end up regretting it. You mark my words,
it's only a matter of time before these women get hurt or killed, or get
somebody else hurt or killed. That Churchill's an idiot."

Not having been very long in police work, I couldn't understand my
partner's adamant opposition to having policewomen on patrol. Police
work, I'd discovered in my short time on the department, wasn't a "lone
wolf" occupation. Police officers helped each other constantly. Although
in 1969 most police officers on the Indianapolis Police Department patrolled in one-officer cars, the dispatchers always sent two cars on runs
that might have any level of danger connected to them. And police offi-

cers, if they had to fight someone, didn't, as often seen in the movies, go one on one. If it took three officers to subdue someone, we used three; if it took five officers, we used five. I had heard that both Liz and Betty weren't shrinking violets, and could more than hold their own. So, with my lack of history at the police department, I really couldn't understand my partner's animosity against them or his certainty that they were a danger to themselves and others.

When we arrived at the address of the run, we saw several police cars already there. So we just waved and passed on by.

"See, what'd I tell you, they've got to have men come by and back them up," my partner grumbled as he drove north on College.

I didn't say anything in response to this, even though in my short experience on the department I'd found that we usually spent much of our shift backing up other police officers.

"All those women are doing is just taking up real policemen's time covering their asses," my partner went on. "That Churchill! What a dumbass!"

⪢

During my first few years at the Indianapolis Police Department, when Car 47 was in its beginnings, I found a wide difference of opinion among the male police officers concerning the value of policewomen on street patrol. Some of the officers, particularly those with ten years or less on the department, supported the program and saw real value in having policewomen on the street. Not only could these women help by patrolling, but there were certain jobs that only policewomen could do, such as searching female prisoners, and some jobs, as discussed previously, that women could do better than men, such as interviewing sexual assault victims and calming children at violent scenes.

However, a number of officers, mostly older officers who had spent their whole careers in the male-only world of police patrol, felt deeply offended by the intrusion of policewomen into their world. The reaction of my partner in the anecdote above was mild compared to the screaming tirades of some of the older officers. Of course, readers must keep in mind that during this period few people thought of women as being equal to men. For example, according to an article in the *Indianapolis*

*Star,* "Before 1971, women weren't even allowed in the garage and pit areas of Indianapolis Motor Speedway; female reporters did interviews through a fence."[1]

"Some guys ignored us, some guys wouldn't speak to us when we spoke to them, and some guys came right out and told us it was the most ridiculous thing they had ever heard of," Liz told me. "The old-timers thought the Chief had lost his mind. They thought that we should stay home and have kids, and not try to do a man's job. Most of the time Betty and I took it all in stride though and usually just smiled. Betty was older than me, and more mature, and occasionally when I got hot about the way some of the guys treated us, she kept me in line. I'd get all mad and upset, and she'd tell me that's not the way to do it."[2]

Of course, this problem of male opposition wasn't unique just to Indianapolis. "The largest obstacle I had to overcome in my career was the attitude of the male officers," former Chief of Police Penny Harrington of Portland, Oregon, told me. "When I began my career in 1964, women were not allowed to be on patrol. We did all of the cases involving women and children. So we were no threat to the men, and they liked to have us there because they hated the 'social work' of dealing with these issues. But then, as we broke into patrol and other units, they immediately took the attitude that women could not do the job. This attitude was not based on facts or events, but just on their bullheaded beliefs."[3]

This assignment of policewomen to certain "social work" cases that policemen didn't want to take was not just a few isolated incidents in just a few police departments, but actually was very prevalent in police departments everywhere, even after policewomen went out on street patrol. "I began my career walking a beat on midnights, as most young officers do," Sergeant Jody Kasper of the Northampton, Massachusetts, Police Department told me. "After a year, I joined the bike patrol in an effort to escape the midnight shift. Three years later, I began working as a detective, where I spent five years and specialized, as all the female detectives before me, in child abuse, sexual assaults, and family crimes."[4]

And, also as in Indianapolis, when policewomen went out on street patrol in other cities, certain older officers could simply never accept this. "On my very first road assignment," retired Chief Montejo of the Miami-Dade Police Department told me, "I had a sergeant who every single day I walked in would say, 'Why don't you go be a teacher? Why don't you go be a nurse? You're taking food away from a man who has a family to raise.' This was a bit unnerving. But to his credit, when it came time for my evaluation at the end of the year he gave me a satisfactory one. It was difficult, though, when you're just starting out, not to have your sergeant supporting you."[5]

Sadly, however, some of the male officers in other police departments, once policewomen on street patrol spread out from Indianapolis, went much further than just verbal abuse such as Chief Montejo suffered. According to news reports, Los Angeles police officer Mark Fuhrman, who came to the public's attention through the O. J. Simpson trial, reportedly once led a group of policemen called Men against Women (MAW). This group allegedly tried to intimidate policewomen into leaving the police department. According to news reports, "The Los Angeles Police Commission's 18-month investigation of the Fuhrman tapes found MAW actually existed in the 1980s, with dozens of members promoting discrimination and intimidation of women in blue." Fuhrman claimed that in its heyday MAW had 145 members.

Along with trying to intimidate policewomen, MAW also reportedly attempted to punish any policemen who fraternized with policewomen by shunning and ostracizing them. The group would hold mock trials for officers believed to be friendly with female officers. Allegedly, Fuhrman even claimed that he put his own partner on trial for talking to a policewoman.[6]

In a 1987 study of the Los Angeles Police Department, 76 percent of the female officers said that they were subject to sexist remarks. In addition to this, 70 percent of the female officers also reported that they were not judged on ability, 55 percent reported having partners who told them they were incompetent, and 43 percent were confronted with a "lack of sensitivity to cultural/racial issues."[7]

Matters involving policewomen at the Los Angeles Police Department eventually became so hostile that, in 1991, Joseph Wambaugh, the highly successful author and former Los Angeles police officer, recommended that a woman be made the chief of police and that the Los Angeles Police Department be made up of 50 percent women because "female cops can go a long way toward helping to mitigate the super-aggressive, paramilitary, macho myth of the gung ho cop and introducing the sobering element of maturity in police work." He then went on to add, "Police work is not about physical altercations . . . [or] about shooting people. . . . It's about talking to people and problem solving, tasks for which women are eminently better qualified than men."[8]

Along with the reluctance of many policemen to accept policewomen as equals on street patrol, the attitude of many of these policemen didn't improve much when policewomen began moving from street patrol into other previously male-only police jobs. "There's a lot of good ol' boys that kind of didn't feel I needed to be there because of the type of work they do—high-risk search warrants and things like that," said Columbia County (South Carolina) Sheriff's Deputy Judy Thomason, who is now a canine handler and boasts that she is the team's first female member.[9]

"I was assigned to Homicide," Chief Montejo told me, "and the female detective there before me had passed out at one of her crime scenes, so when I came in they were watching closely to see what I would do. My first crime scene was a suicide, and when I started my investigation, the guys said, 'Hey, stick your finger in the bullet hole so we can get a clearer crime scene picture.' I'm thinking, 'Well, there goes my crime scene,' but I knew exactly what they were doing. So I stuck my finger in the bullet hole, and they were like, 'Well, that's sure not what we expected.' But they got it, and after that I had a very good working relationship in Homicide, and that was at a time when we didn't have a lot of women in specialized units. Working there helped build my credibility in the department, and I think I got a lot of new opportunities based on my performance in Homicide."[10]

However, it wasn't just the many policemen and police administrators across the country who opposed the idea of policewomen on street patrol and in other previously male-only police jobs. Often the public didn't agree with the idea either. In a letter sent by Betty to Liz, who was on vacation in October 1970, Betty tells of an encounter with a citizen who obviously didn't believe policewomen should be on the street.

"I had the street blocked with my car for a raid," Betty wrote. "Some little guy in an MG from Van Nuys, California, wanted to take exception to us having the street blocked. 'Excuse me,' he said when saw me, 'I thought you were the real police.'"[11]

Assistant Chief Susan Bretthauer of the Stamford, Connecticut, Police Department has a very similar story. "One time, after a business owner's alarm went off, he told the female officer who arrived on the scene that he wanted to see her supervisor, so the sergeant came—but she was also a female, so he demanded to see her supervisor. That's when I showed up."[12]

Sergeant Amy Adams of the New Hanover County, North Carolina, Sheriff's Office knows just how these policewomen felt. "A lot of people at crime scenes look at the guys and say, 'That's your supervisor?'" she said. "It's changing, but people still sometimes automatically look for a man to be in charge of a scene."[13]

Chief Montejo told me:

> Early on, the public snubbed me occasionally because I was a female. In the 1970s, female officers were a kind of novelty. I went on a call once where a man refused to talk to me. It was just a neighborhood dispute, and when I walked up, he said, "I'm not talking to you. I want a real cop." I said, "Well, this is what you're getting. I am a real cop." He said, "Nope, I want to talk to a man." I said, "Okay, see ya," and I left. Then he called back and I got the call. We went through this three times, and finally he said, "Are you like the only cop working today?" I said, "Yeah, I am, so you're going to have to talk to me or you're not getting the report taken." So he gave me the information.
>
> This kind of thing didn't happen very often, but occasionally someone at a call would say, "Oh look, here comes a girl." It was very frustrating.[14]

Unfortunately, like many policemen and some members of the public, the command staffs of many police departments, even though fighting a national trend, also often didn't approve of policewomen on street patrol. They would many times try to do all they could to discourage policewomen from transferring there. In October 1981, for example, the chief of police of Knoxville, Tennessee, ordered all of the policewomen on street patrol to cut their hair short like the men's. Chief Robert Marshall told the women, "This is a tough job. This is not a place to look pretty."[15] The Tennessee Association of Women Police vowed to fight that order.

In Philadelphia in the 1970s, policewomen on street patrol were not allowed to ride in police vehicles with policemen. "The females were not assigned to the cars with males," said former Philadelphia police officer Pat Brennan. "They were afraid we were going to have sex in the car."

Also according to Brennan, policewomen in 1970s Philadelphia could choose to switch from street patrol to being juvenile aid officers and earn the same pay as regular police officers. But first, they had to sign a document saying that women were not qualified to be police officers.[16]

As another example, the Nassau County Police Department in New York reportedly quickly invented new rules when policewomen on street patrol began getting promoted. Now Chief of Detectives Joan Yale recalls one of these quickly invented rules: "Under no circumstances could a female supervise a male or work after midnight."[17]

Along with police department command staffs, male street supervisors also often tried to do all they could to discourage policewomen from seeking positions on street patrol. In 1972, in Wilmington, North Carolina, newly hired policewoman Martha Lanier Currie got into a scuffle with a drunk. Suddenly, several men came out of a nearby bar and began threatening her. As any police officer would do in such a situation, she radioed for assistance.

"And the lieutenant came on the radio and said, 'Don't go to her aid, let her fight it out herself,'" Currie later recalled. "He didn't like females in patrol, didn't want them, and was trying his best to get me to leave. I was determined not to."[18]

Fortunately, a nearby policeman ignored the lieutenant's order and came to Currie's assistance, and the crowd quickly dispersed. The lieutenant, outraged, immediately suspended the policeman for three days without pay.

Police officer Mary Kulgren of the Seattle Police Department recalls her field training in 1977: "The lieutenant that was in charge of the student officers told me he was going to do anything he could to fire me because he didn't think women should be on the police department."[19] He wasn't successful, however.

Even though Liz and Betty in Indianapolis had the unqualified support of the chief, they didn't immediately win the full acceptance of the rest of the police department staff. The two women especially had difficulty with one dispatcher (who in those days were all older male police officers). This dispatcher seemed determined to make them quit.

"One time, this certain dispatcher, in order to test us, gave us a run to shoot a sick dog," Liz told me. "That was part of the police job at that time. Betty and I went to the scene and found this really sick dog. He was foaming at the mouth. So I took out the shotgun and shot him. The dispatcher couldn't believe it, and made us call him to confirm that we had really shot the dog. He really didn't think we could handle it."[20]

Liz also told me of another time this same dispatcher tried to sabotage them. "When we first got out onto the street we were trying to keep a low profile until we could get the guys used to us," Liz said. "One day, Betty and I pulled behind a car that was weaving back and forth and driving real slow. It was obvious the driver was drunk. But when we turned on the lights and siren he wouldn't stop. He didn't speed up or try to get away. He just kept weaving at a slow speed.

"We told the dispatcher that we were not in a chase, but that the car just wouldn't stop. The dispatcher, though, immediately broadcasted on both channels that Car 47 was in a chase, and needed help. Every minute or two he would update our location, which would be about a hundred feet from the last location. His announcement brought police cars from all around.

"Fortunately, the guy finally pulled into a tavern parking lot, and seemed really surprised by all the police cars. He was totally drunk. The whole situation was really bad because the dispatcher had made it look like we'd panicked. But still, it also made us feel good to see all of the officers who came to help us."[21]

When I talked to Betty's daughter, Robin, about her mother's experiences on the street, she told me,

> There were a lot of mixed feelings. There were some guys who left them hanging on runs to see if they could handle it. But then too some guys thought it was a good idea to have policewomen on the street, and that they could be utilized to everyone's benefit. Others, though, would go to great lengths to sabotage them. Mom and Liz decided to just ignore them, and go on and do the job. Mom and Liz were very resourceful women and figured out how to work around these obstacles. Because they could talk to people, they found they could usually talk their way out of difficult situations. They used being female to their advantage in volatile situations.
>
> They also devised a system when they went out onto the street. Liz would drive and Mom would handle the radio. If they got a runner, Liz's job was to get her gun out of her purse, kick off her high heels, and chase the suspect. Mom's job was to retrieve Liz's purse and shoes, jump into

the car, and head in the direction Liz was running. She'd then either try to box the suspect in or force him to double back toward Liz.

Mom told me that many times she would round the corner and see Liz straddled on top of a suspect face down on the ground, trying to make sure her backside wasn't exposed to onlookers (the glory of skirts). Mom wasn't a runner, and Liz was great at running. Mom usually handled the radio, although she told me they rarely ever put anything out on the radio until it was all over. They didn't want to become known as wimpy women who always needed help. Mom also told me that she couldn't remember a time when she and Liz couldn't make the apprehension by themselves someway. Mom, like Liz, could handle herself during any confrontations.

They always talked things out between them and had a plan of who was going to do what if plan A went bad. Above all, they trusted each other literally with their lives because they came to realize quickly that they had to depend on each other if they were going to be able to stay out on the street, which was their ultimate goal. After I joined the police department in 1990, a lot of the old-timers would tell me that if they ever heard Liz and Mom calling for help they raced toward their location because they knew they were in trouble since they hardly ever asked for help.[22]


Naturally, after Car 47 proved successful in Indianapolis, other cities across the country began being pressured to institute their own female patrol programs, and many cities did. However, as discussed previously, policewomen in other cities, even after Indianapolis had shown that women could do the job of street patrol, still faced many of the same reactions from the older officers that Car 47 did.

Interestingly, one of the major complaints that many policemen originally had about policewomen on street patrol was that, because they are smaller than men, women are less intimidating, and consequently will have to resort to force more often than men. However, a research project published in 2005 reported on a seven-year study of the Montgomery County, Maryland, Police Department, which during the time of the study was 18.6 percent female. The study found no significant difference in the use of force by male and female officers.[23]

Although much of the reaction to female officers we have talked about in this chapter took place in the 1960s and 1970s, the acceptance of policewomen didn't become universal after that. Unfortunately, even after women showed over and over in police departments all across the country that they could do the job of police patrol, many men continued to believe that women have no place in policing.

In 1980 a researcher concluded that "negative male attitudes toward women in law enforcement have been the most significant factor in hindering the advancement of policewomen. No solid proof supports this male bias against policewomen, but none is needed, since males run the police departments."[24]

More recently, in February 1997, according to an article in the *New York Times*, South Hackensack, New York, turned down a $375,000 federal grant to hire five new police officers. The reason? According to Chief of Police Joseph Brown, it was because the top person on the eligibility list was a woman, and the township officials did not want to hire a woman.[25]

Amazingly, in June 2007 an article appeared in the magazine *Law and Order* suggesting that policemen and policewomen should be trained separately. Even though in the article the authors put forth various reasons for their support of this idea, I can't believe that many policewomen working under such a system would consider themselves as being equal with the policemen.[26]

As a consequence of this continued resistance from many individuals to the idea of gender equality in police departments, many policewomen feel pressured to prove over and over that they can handle the job. As late as 2004, a policewoman told a newspaper reporter, "As a female you feel as though you have to prove yourself a little more as far as being able to handle an arrest. Or if you get into some sort of physical altercation—you want to make sure that your counterpart or your peers feel as though you are going to take care of business just as well as they are."[27]

"When I started out 17 years ago it was definitely a challenge being a woman," said Master Police Officer Beth Lavin of the King County, Washington, Sheriff's Office in 2008, "because you feel like you have to go out there and fight with somebody to prove to the guys you can handle yourself and you're not 'one of those wimpy female officers.'"[28]

"I certainly have noticed differences in male and female officers over the years," Sergeant Jody Kasper told me in 2009. "These differences have little to do with actual police work on the street and more to do with the differences in the way women are perceived by male officers and how women perceive themselves. I believe that as women we are constantly challenged to do more and do better in a career-long effort to prove ourselves. And yet, this need to prove ourselves, while on-going year after year for female officers, is usually only a short, introductory period for men when they first come on the job."[29]

But some policewomen feel as though they will never be able to prove themselves to the policemen. "No matter how often a woman proves herself in the job, she's got to do it over and over again," said Diane Skoog, executive director of the National Association of Women Law Enforcement Executives (NAWLEE) and the former chief of police for the Carver, Massachusetts, Police Department. "Once a guy does it, he's set."[30]

Fortunately, policewomen across the country persevered in their struggle for equality and were able to gain and maintain a foothold in previously male-only territory. Of course, once it finally became clear to most male police officers and law enforcement administrators that their struggle to stop policewomen from going on street patrol and into other previously male-only police jobs was very likely futile, a new problem for policewomen, often borne of male frustration at being unable to stop the advance of policewomen, then emerged: sexual harassment. Although we will cover this subject in detail in the next chapter, this was, and still is, a serious problem for policewomen. In one study, for example, a researcher found that 63 percent of the policewomen interviewed in five large metropolitan police departments reported instances of sexual harassment on the job, including 25 percent who had experienced *quid pro quo* sexual harassment.[31]

Although not sexual harassment per se, another interesting problem for policewomen I saw often during my thirty-eight years as a police officer is that many people, including those in the media, tend to judge the actions of policewomen differently than the same actions of policemen. Mistakes that policemen made all the time with no consequences are often considered fatal flaws for policewomen. Officer Joanne Hunt of the Seattle Police Department, who was one of the first nine policewomen to go on street patrol there in 1976, said, "When you'd hear a story about somebody really screwing up you'd go, 'Please, God, don't let it be a woman.' That feeling is something you can't get away from because as a woman if you screw up it reflects on all the women, but if a white male screws up it's just him."[32]

A good example of this tendency to judge policewomen with a different standard than policemen, and an example that shows that this tendency continues well into the twenty-first century, is the case of Brian Nichols. On November 11, 2005, Nichols, a man on his way to court to be tried for rape, overpowered a female deputy escorting him and took her gun. He then killed three people in the courthouse, including a judge. Nichols afterward escaped from the courthouse and went on a crime spree, eventually killing a U.S. Customs and Immigration agent. The police captured Nichols the next day. Many people criticized the fact that a lone woman was escorting this very dangerous criminal. I agree with that criticism, not because the officer was a woman, but because for some reason a supervisor had allowed a dangerous criminal to be escorted by a lone officer. There should have been two officers.

Many people, however, including those in the media, didn't see the problem of a lone officer escorting a dangerous criminal, but instead focused on the fact that it was a woman who had escorted Nichols. They focused on their belief that, because she was a woman, she was weak and ineffectual and Nichols was able to overpower her and take her gun. These people obviously believed that this wouldn't have happened to a man. However, these people are obviously unaware that 10 percent of the policemen who are killed every year by firearms are killed with their own guns, which some criminal took away from them. But you never hear complaints about these policemen being weak and ineffectual.

Also in the Nichols case, a picture in the media of Nichols' capture the next day shows him being escorted to a waiting police car by a female police officer. This raised a firestorm of criticism on Michelle Malkin's website at michellemalkin.com.

One person wrote, "The killer of an Atlanta judge is shown being taken into custody by a woman cop, after the same killer took a gun away from a woman court cop to go on his killing spree. Isn't there something wrong with this photo?"

Another person said, "People have warned for years that female law enforcement personnel could put people at risk because they may not be able to subdue a dangerous defendant. Because of the physical mismatch, a defendant could overpower the female officer and take her gun. Well, this is exactly what happened. Another way in which the PC agenda kills people."[33]

An interesting point that many people who wrote in to this website didn't seem to catch is that this is not a single policewoman escorting the captured Nichols to the police car. She has her arm on Nichols, but several male officers can also be seen in the picture.

Author Ann Coulter also weighed in on this case with an article titled, "Freeze! I Just Had My Nails Done!" Readers can imagine her position from the title of the article.[34]

As a police officer who has worked with many policewomen during my career, I know that it takes a special type of woman to be a good police officer, and that not every woman (or man) has the capability or courage to become one. However, just because a woman like Coulter feels that there is no way *she* could do the job is no reason to insist that *no* woman can do it.

Of course, the problem of resistance to policewomen on street patrol and in other previously male-only police jobs isn't a problem just confined to the United States. Klara Homolacova, a policewoman in Prague, Czechoslovakia, talked to a reporter in 2005 about the attitude of policemen toward her. "Their attitude was pretty straightforward and clear—there is no place for a woman in the police. . . . Male colleagues would for example slam the door in front of me just like students in schools tend to do. I was even thinking of leaving at one stage but I am glad I didn't."[35]

In a survey in 2007 of the female officers on the Royal Canadian Mounted Police, only a minority of women felt that "everyone is treated fairly."[36] As another example of the resistance to policewomen in previously male-only positions, in November 2007, an order went out from the Interior Ministry in Iraq, which oversees the police, for all policewomen in Iraq to turn in their weapons, apparently in an attempt to force the women to take administrative posts. This, of course, raised a furor, and, in January 2008, the ministry rescinded the order.

Even though, as we've seen, for many years policemen and law enforcement administrators vigorously opposed putting policewomen on street patrol, police departments have nevertheless reaped huge benefits from it. Data from several studies show that policewomen account for only 5 percent of all citizen allegations of excessive force and only 2 percent of the sustained allegations. In addition, policewomen account for only 6 percent of the dollars police departments pay out each year in settlements and court judgments for excessive force. And even in those cases in which the actions of policewomen do result in excessive-force settlements and court judgments, the dollar amounts are 2½ to 5½ times smaller than for policemen.[37]

To further demonstrate this advantage of having female police officers on street patrol, a study in Los Angeles found that from 1990 to 1999 the city paid out $63.4 million in lawsuit settlements and judgments against policemen for excessive force. Yet, during this same period, the city paid out only $2.8 million in lawsuit settlements and judgments against policewomen for excessive force, a 23:1 difference, even though the male/female ratio was just 4:1.

A similar study in Cincinnati found that the difference in excessive-force settlement and judgment payouts between policemen and police-women was 12:1. The male/female officer ratio during the study was just 5:1.[38]

Interestingly, however, even with these differences in excessive force payouts, several research projects have shown that in the lower levels of force used by police officers there is no difference in the number of use-of-force incidents between policemen and policewomen. It is only when the level of force used by officers escalates to the top end of the use-of-force continuum that the use by policemen seriously outnumbers the use by policewomen. The Christopher Commission, which looked into the use of excessive force by Los Angeles police officers following the Rodney King incident, summed it up by saying, "Female officers are not reluctant to use force but they are not nearly as likely to be involved in [the] use of excessive force."[39]

Although some readers might argue that these statistics only come about because policewomen don't work as hard or perform as well as policemen, studies also dispute this claim. In 1974, the Police Foundation issued a report that detailed a study conducted by the Urban Institute of Washington, D.C. This study compared the yearlong work records of eighty-six policemen and eighty-six policewomen assigned to street patrol in Washington, D.C. The researchers concluded:

> The men and women studied for this report performed patrol work in a generally similar manner. They responded to similar types of calls for police service while on patrol and encountered similar proportions of citi-

zens who were dangerous, angry, upset, drunk, or violent. Both men and women officers were observed to obtain similar results in handling angry or violent citizens. There were no reported incidents [that] cast serious doubt on the ability of women to perform patrol work satisfactorily, and in fact this study includes reports of some incidents in which individual women performed quite well in difficult circumstances.[40]

Researchers later conducted similar studies in St. Louis, New York City, and Denver, all with similar findings.

Another study of policewomen found no difference in the crime rates, clearance rates, cost of operations, or citizen satisfaction rates between agencies with low numbers of female officers and agencies with high numbers of female officers.[41] What all of these reports found is what I have observed during my long career: women can be excellent police officers. Policewomen, I've found, simply use different tactics than policemen, but are still able to very successfully handle tough assignments and unruly people.

Fresno, California, Police Sergeant Marty True had this to say about policewomen and confrontational and unruly people: "I think [female officers] recognize their physical limitations and don't rely on strength to control suspects; they primarily rely on talking their way through situations."[42]

Chief Montejo told me:

Different doesn't make it wrong. Policewomen do things a little differently. We don't usually have the physical strength that the male officers do, so we have to use different tactics. And we're very successful at it. Police departments find that the use of force and complaint numbers go down when they begin hiring women.[43]

This technique of verbal persuasion works for policewomen because of an interesting truth that I quickly discovered as a young police officer: very few confrontational or unruly people—probably 1 percent or less— really want to fight. Everyone wants to bluster and talk a good game, but very few people really want to get physical. Every policeman has had the experience many times of dealing with confrontational citizens who shout and bluster about how they'll kick the ass of every police officer standing around, but after getting themselves physically thrown into the police car and driven away from their friends, will suddenly begin crying and pleading with the officer not to arrest them.

Policewomen, on the other hand, simply handle these people by allowing them to bluster in front of their friends and then, rather than physically forcing them into the police car, persuade them to voluntarily get into the car, which these individuals do because they really don't want to fight anyway. However, according to the many policewomen I've talked to, once away from their friends, these individuals still usually cry and plead not go to jail. In actuality, this tactic used by policewomen is much better overall for police departments because it results in fewer complaints of excessive force.

Although in this chapter I've given a very negative picture of many of the male officers' attitudes about policewomen on street patrol, I don't want readers to think that every male officer felt totally opposed to the idea. Liz told me that a small number of male officers welcomed them and tried to do their best to help her and Betty acclimate to street patrol.

A quote from an article in the April 1975 issue of *Ladies Home Journal* shows that, even early in the history of policewomen on street patrol, not all male officers opposed the idea. "In Dayton, Captain H. G. Reed, Sr., a 35-year veteran of the force, never thought he'd see the day women were on patrol. 'My first reaction was,' he said, 'it'll never work. I was scared. But I was willing to try it.' Now Captain Reed is a staunch supporter of women, even in command positions."[44]

We've talked a lot in this chapter about the historical resistance of policemen to women officers on street patrol, but has time changed the attitudes of policemen? The University of South Florida conducted two studies concerning the attitudes of policemen about women officers, one in 1976 and the other in 1994. The studies took place at the Tampa Police Department, the St. Petersburg Police Department, and the Hillsborough County Sheriff's Office. In 1976 only 15.8 percent of the male officers felt that policewomen were as effective as policemen. In 1994, this had increased to 59.4 percent. In 1976, 58.4 percent of the male officers felt that policewomen could not handle violent situations. In 1994, this had dropped to 17.8 percent. And finally, in 1976 only 27.9 percent of the male officers said that they wouldn't mind working with a female officer. In 1994, this had risen to 70.8 percent.[45]

This growth in the acceptance of policewomen also applies to the general public, many of whom also didn't immediately approve of the idea of policewomen on street patrol. In the March 1997 issue of the *American Journal of Criminal Justice,* Kristen Leger of the University of Louisville tells of a study conducted to test the public's acceptance of policewomen on street patrol. What she found was that the public does indeed now generally accept the idea that policewomen are equal to policemen.[46]

Even though, as we've seen in this chapter, many policemen and law enforcement administrators vigorously opposed the use of policewomen on street patrol and in other previously male-only police jobs, programs across the country still continued to grow. Nevertheless, some policemen and police administrators weren't to be swayed, and many times, as we will see in the next chapter, they took desperate—and often illegal— actions in an attempt to discourage policewomen from serving in positions previously considered "male-only."

# HEROINES IN THE
# STRUGGLE FOR EQUALITY

**O**n December 4, 1971, the city of Chicago administered its entrance exam for patrol officers with the Chicago Police Department. However, indicative of the times, the city restricted the test to men only. Women had to apply in June of the next year, and then could apply only for certain female-specific jobs within the police department, including policewoman and matron. Also indicative of the times, the policewoman position did not include street patrol. In June 1972, these gender-specific requirements forced Barbara McNamara, who had always dreamed of being a police officer like Liz and Betty, to take the policewoman/police matron exam if she wanted to be a member of the Chicago Police Department.

In April 1972, Title VII of the Civil Rights Act of 1964 became applicable to municipalities. The city of Chicago, however, ignored this law's requirements and continued to hire its male police officers from the 1971 list and its female employees from the 1972 list. On November 7, 1974, a federal district court issued a preliminary injunction against the city of Chicago that prohibited it from using the 1971 exam results. On February 2, 1976, the federal district court then issued a permanent injunction that required the city of Chicago to hire women on an equal basis with men.

Regardless of these court orders, in March 1976 the city of Chicago hired McNamara based on her scores from the 1972 test. McNamara consequently sued the Chicago Police Department for back pay and seniority from April 3, 1972, the date Title VII took effect in municipalities. She argued that if the city of Chicago had not discriminated against women by closing the exam for patrol officer to them she would have been hired long before her actual hire date in 1976.

A federal district court, on March 30, 1987, found in McNamara's favor. The court awarded her $36,666.24 in back pay from 1972, retroactive seniority from then, attorney fees, and $67,758.80 in prejudgment interest. The city of Chicago appealed.

The Seventh Circuit Court of Appeals heard the case on February 12, 1988, and issued its decision in McNamara's favor on August 3, 1988. The court concluded, "Accordingly, the district court's ruling, in all respects, is affirmed."[1]

Many policewomen over the years, along with Officer McNamara, have found themselves facing an entrenched bureaucracy seemingly set up to oppose their entry into police departments, or their ability to gain equality with the men once there. These women have discovered that often the only way they can gain entry into a police department or establish a level of equality with the male officers once inside is through a lawsuit.

For example, in the 1970s a number of police departments, in an attempt to keep women out, began establishing height and weight requirements that would exclude many women. In 1976, Diane Rawlinson, a twenty-two-year-old college graduate with a degree in correctional psychology, applied for a position as a correctional counselor in Alabama. However, the state of Alabama rejected her for the position because she was five-foot-three, but weighed only 115 pounds, and consequently did not meet the state minimum that had been set for applicants of five-foot-two and 120 pounds. She and another woman, Brenda Meith, who had been turned down for similar reasons when she applied to be an Alabama state trooper, filed a lawsuit, claiming that the height and weight requirements set by the state of Alabama discriminated against women.

The trial court in *Dothard v. Rawlinson* found in favor of the women. The state of Alabama appealed the case to the U.S. Supreme Court, which also found in the women's favor, ruling that height and weight requirements did indeed discriminate against women.[2] As a result, one huge roadblock for women attempting to enter law enforcement had been removed.

However, many police departments refused to be deterred in their fight to keep women out of police departments, and they came up with a new way to discourage female applicants: rigorous physical agility tests. Because many police departments today still use these physical agility tests, even though their requirements often have no basis in research or reality, we will talk more about them in the next chapter.

In the 1970s and 1980s, because so many women sued police departments that tried to keep them out, the courts began imposing sanctions against police departments in the form of consent decrees for female applicants. A consent decree essentially says that every recruit class a police department has must contain a certain percentage of women until the police department reaches a target percentage of policewomen in the department. In many cases, if a police department couldn't get their percentage of women in a recruit class, there would be no recruit class.

A study of 282 police agencies reported by the National Center for Women & Policing in 2000 provided some interesting statistics about the effectiveness of consent decrees. Of the twenty-five police agencies studied with the highest percentage of policewomen, ten were under consent decrees; only four of the twenty-five police departments with the lowest percentage of policewomen were under consent decrees. In police departments without consent decrees, women accounted for an average of 9.7 percent of the department; in police departments with consent decrees, women made up an average of 14 percent of the department.[3]

I was in charge of the Indianapolis Police Department's Personnel Branch for six years while we, even though a forerunner in the advancement of policewomen, were, embarrassingly, under a consent decree to hire women. I found that a consent decree makes the police department work harder to find qualified female applicants. While without a consent decree we might have simply put out a recruitment notice and waited to see who showed up, under the consent decree the police department sent recruitment officers to women's colleges, job fairs for women, and other places where qualified women might be found.

A good case that shows just how well a consent decree works is that of Pittsburgh. At the time their consent decree went into effect, women accounted for only 1 percent of the Pittsburgh Police Department. Before the consent decree expired, they had 27.2 percent women.[4]

Sometimes, however, matters of equality for women don't involve hiring standards or the numbers of policewomen, but instead involve simple human needs. For example, in 2007 several policewomen of the Saratoga Springs, New York, Police Department filed a workplace discrimination lawsuit. Only one woman at a time, they claimed, could change in the tiny woman's locker room, and there were no bathrooms specifically for policewomen, although there were for policemen. In January 2008, the New York Division of Human Rights upheld their grievance and ordered the Saratoga Springs Police Department to provide bathrooms and showers for its female officers.[5]

Unfortunately, sometimes policewomen have found that discipline can also be meted out differently for policewomen and policemen who violate the same rule. On November 19, 2001, Albuquerque policewoman Sheryl Paloni and her partner, Officer Paulette Mashburn, shot at the tires of a car holding a fleeing bank robber, an act in violation of Albuquerque Police Department policy. (This action isn't allowed in many police departments, except in situations of life and death, because of the danger of ricochets.) A male officer, however, also shot at the fleeing car's tires. Afterward, Paloni and Mashburn received discipline for the incident, but the male officer didn't. Paloni filed a complaint with the Equal Employment Opportunity Commission (EEOC), and the commission found in her and her partner's favor, stating that the discipline had been discriminatory.

"It was great to see that they saw this really obvious violation," Paloni said of the ruling.[6]

Along with all of the problems talked about so far, often policewomen have also found that, even after they have managed to gain entry onto a police force as patrol officers, transfers and promotions can be routinely denied to them because of their sex. Again, these women have many times faced an entrenched bureaucracy with rules set up to keep them from advancing within the department. Consequently, these women have often been forced to look to the courts for help.

In 1994, Nina Acosta, who worked in the Los Angeles Police Department's Metro Division, tried out for a coveted SWAT team position. She passed all of the intense fitness tests, but still wasn't selected to enter the SWAT training program to become a part of the unit.

"There could have been only one reason and that was because I was a woman," Acosta said on a National Public Radio interview. "I did very well in the tryouts. And when we got the tapes, because they tape the whole process, it proved exactly what I knew all along, that I had beaten most of the guys in the head to head competition."

Acosta also said that the lieutenant in charge was "very arrogant about saying women do not belong in SWAT." She said he told her, "You guys can work in the field and work in juvenile detectives or work the front desk and all that stuff, but SWAT's where all the men play."[7]

This naturally upset Acosta and so she sued. A Superior Court jury agreed with her, and they awarded her $2.3 million in damages. As a consequence of the lawsuit, the Los Angeles Police Department has finally allowed policewomen to be accepted into its SWAT training program.

Sometimes, however, it is not a coveted assignment that police departments try to keep women out of, but instead certain high ranks that will give women input into the police department's top management decisions. For example, in 1996 the United States Department of Justice sued Canton, Mississippi, because they refused to promote Lieutenant Vickie McNeill to the position of assistant chief, even though she ranked as the most qualified. According to a Department of Justice press release, "After investigating, the EEOC found that she was the most qualified person for the position and found evidence that some of those who made the hiring decision believed that a woman was unable to fulfill the duties of Assistant Chief of Police."[8] The city of Canton eventually relented and promoted Lieutenant McNeill to Assistant Chief.

This situation, incidentally, is by no means confined to Canton, Mississippi. A female officer interviewed by a researcher stated,

> The promotional process for sergeant is pretty specific and it is difficult not to promote the individuals who score well. However, our agency has not promoted females into command staff level. While there are four female

sergeants (out of 25 sergeants), there are only two lieutenants. There aren't any sworn females holding any rank above lieutenant. The promotional process for captain and above is done by interviews and it is discouraging that no females are being promoted to higher ranks. Our department has 240 sworn officers and only six females in positions of rank.[9]

Often, however, even when women manage through a lawsuit or other means to attain certain ranks or coveted positions within a police department, there are those who resent their success so much that they harass them. Officer Beth Kreuzer, for example, became the first policewoman to be assigned to the Houston Police Department's elite motorcycle unit. Upon her arrival at the unit, a supervisor began harassing her in ways that included insensitive comments and inappropriate touching. When she complained, she was both surprised and delighted to find that her shift of officers backed the complaint. However, soon afterward, several members of the police department allegedly began retaliating against the entire shift. In 2005, a jury awarded Officer Kreuzer $600,000.

Sadly, once it became apparent to the male officers on many police departments across the United States that they couldn't stop policewomen from requesting and getting jobs previously held only by men, some of these policemen resorted to sexual harassment tactics in an attempt to make the women feel so uncomfortable that they would leave. Many times the administrations of some police departments were either involved in this sexual harassment or simply allowed it to continue without interference. The courts, however, took a very dim view of this behavior and often punished these offenders and police departments severely.

There are two types of sexual harassment that occur within police departments. The first is *quid pro quo* harassment, in which a tangible benefit is contingent upon submission to unwanted sexual advances. The second type is hostile sexual harassment, in which individuals use sexual comments, inappropriate touching, the posting of pornography in open areas, sexually oriented e-mails, and so on to make the workplace intolerable for women.

In studies of various police departments, often as many as 63 to 68 percent of the policewomen interviewed report having experienced sexual harassment, although only 4 to 6 percent of these policewomen have reported the acts. A study by the International Association of Chiefs of Police found that policewomen have won more than one-third of all the sexual harassment lawsuits they have filed against police departments, and that police agencies across the nation have spent hundreds of millions of dollars to settle these lawsuits.[10]

Occasionally, however, while sexual harassment can often be blatant and hostile, it can also at times be subtle. When I headed the Field Training Officer (FTO) Program at the Indianapolis Police Department, a female officer who had just graduated from the program asked to see me. She told me that she hadn't wanted to complain while she was in the program because she just wanted to get through it, but she said that one of the FTOs had asked all of the female officer trainees who rode with him if their bras and panties matched. She said this FTO would give these female officers a good score on organizational skills if they said yes and a poor score if they said no or refused to answer him.

I immediately called the officer in and asked him about this accusation. He admitted doing it, but then tried to justify his actions by explaining his belief that a matching bra and panties showed that a woman had good organizational skills. I asked him if he inquired of the men who rode with him if their underwear and socks matched. At first he seemed dumbfounded, but then said no. I suspended him without pay and recommended his removal from the program.

Many times, however, sexual harassment isn't subtle at all, and, as the following anecdote shows, continues to this day. In November 2008, a jury awarded three female detectives on the Nassau County, New York, Police Department $1 million for emotional damages suffered because of sexual harassment. Reportedly, some of the male officers posted pornography in the precinct, asked the women about their sexual practices, and sent them sexually oriented e-mails.

"It was like a frat house with a boy's club mentality," said retired Nassau County Detective Deirdre Ketchum.[11]

Interestingly, sexual harassers of policewomen aren't always employees of the police department. A bizarre case of sexual harassment in which the perpetrators were not police employees occurred in King County, Washington. Two policewomen at the scene of a meth lab investigation were ordered to strip in a nearby parking lot and use portable showers. This was a safety precaution because of the possibility that they had been exposed to dangerous chemicals. Although the local fire department put up privacy shields for the policewomen, who incidentally hadn't even entered the building where the meth lab was, and therefore had only a very minute chance of being contaminated, the firemen left a gap where four of them watched the policewomen shower.

In July 1996, a jury awarded the two policewomen $105,000 each because of the harassment. In addition, the fire department disciplined the firemen involved. "I think it would be an understatement to say [the policewomen] were exceedingly humiliated by the experience," said the local police guild attorney Chris Vick.[12]

This may seem to some readers to be a bizarre, isolated case that probably needn't be included in our discussion since it is unlikely to happen often, but unfortunately that's not true. Similar instances of voyeurism against policewomen have occurred elsewhere. In December 2006, a court convicted two public officials in Pennsylvania in a case that involved the placement of a hidden video camera in a police department locker room used by policewomen. The two officials, as their defense, claimed that they put the camera there to gather evidence of police officers sleeping on the job. However, instead of videotaping police officers sleeping, they recorded a policewoman disrobing. During their investigation of the case detectives found pornographic material in the desk of one of the officials charged, casting serious doubt on the defense's explanation for the camera's placement.

We talked earlier in this chapter about how 63 to 68 percent of policewomen report having experienced sexual harassment, but also how only 4 to 6 percent of these women report it. This may seem to many readers to be an incredibly small percentage who report sexual harassment violations, and admittedly many likely don't report it for fear of the repercussions, which we will talk about later in this chapter. Some policewomen, however, rather than report sexual harassment, would rather handle the situation on their own. Chief Montejo told me,

> I did experience a bit a sexual harassment back in the 70s. My squad just didn't want to have a female on it. It was minor stuff, though, compared to some of my friends. I think having a sense of humor and not taking everything as a personal attack helped me get through. I used to do a lot

of "drawing a line in the sand," though, and letting people know what was acceptable and unacceptable behavior.[13]

Along with sexual harassment, many policewomen have also faced serious opposition within police departments when it comes to maternity issues. This problem occurs because, while many women join a police department because they want to have a career in law enforcement, many of these women also want to have a family and consequently become pregnant. Unfortunately, many of these policewomen have quickly discovered that some police departments are less than accommodating, often forcing them to use their sick leave, vacation time, or unpaid leave during their pregnancies. Occasionally, policewomen have even been forced to resign if they want to have children. And, although male police officers with temporary disabilities can request and often receive light-duty assignments, police departments have routinely denied such requests to pregnant policewomen. Again, it took a number of court battles before police departments finally realized that they needed to accommodate pregnant policewomen.

In June 2006, a jury in New York found in favor of six policewomen on the Suffolk County Police Department. The women sued because the police department had refused to give them light-duty assignments during their pregnancies, and instead forced them to take sick leave and vacation time. In January 2007, Suffolk County signed a consent decree that requires the police department to allow pregnant policewomen six months of light-duty assignment.

In Louisiana, a police department went even further in their hostility toward pregnant policewomen. The Louisiana State Police terminated a female trooper when she reported to them that she was pregnant. She sued and the court found her termination discriminatory. The court ordered her to be reinstated.

Many policewomen, because of extreme employer bias against pregnancy, have been forced to use The Pregnancy Discrimination Act (42 U.S.C. 2000e[k]). This is a federal law that requires employers to treat "women affected by pregnancy, childbirth, or related conditions" the same "as other persons not so affected but similar in their ability to work." This law has been used by many policewomen in suing police departments that have given policemen light-duty assignments for non-duty-related injuries, but then denied these same light-duty assignments to pregnant policewomen.

Charlotte Adams, a police officer with the North Little Rock, Arkansas, Police Department, found herself in just such a situation. She informed her employers that she was pregnant and gave them a letter from her doctor that said she should be put on light duty. When two other policewomen also became pregnant, the police department quickly formulated a policy that said in part,

> Employees who suffer non–work related injury or illness that results in temporary disability, including pregnancy, miscarriage, abortion, childbirth, and recovery thereof, will be granted use of accumulated sick leave, vacation leave, and/or other earned paid time off. Upon expiration of the aforementioned paid leave, the employee must take an unpaid leave of absence if additional time off is needed for recovery.

The police department, however, didn't follow its own policy, and allowed three policemen with non-duty-related injuries to have light-duty assignments. Adams sued the police department. Although a federal district court ruled against her, the 8th Circuit Court of Appeals overturned the ruling, stating, "For the foregoing reasons, we reverse the judgment of the district court and remand with directions to the district court to enter judgment for plaintiff (Adams) against defendant North Little Rock Police Department."[14]

Although pregnant policewomen like Adams have fought to obtain court rulings that give them light-duty assignments, the courts have also ruled against employers in the reverse of this situation. Police departments that discover policewomen are pregnant cannot arbitrarily, or benevolently, move them to light-duty assignments if they don't want to have them. The U.S. Supreme Court decision in *UAW v. Johnson Controls, Inc.* ruled that employers cannot arbitrarily ban pregnant women from hazardous jobs.[15]

In 1998, four female Massachusetts State Troopers sued the state because of one of its policies, which was contrary to *UAW v. Johnson Controls, Inc.* The policy in question stated that troopers who became pregnant could not drive police cruisers, wear the uniform, work overtime, or have contact with prisoners or the public. A jury found in favor of the female troopers, giving the women $347,000 and $1,000,000 in punitive damages. (A jury can award punitive damages if it feels the defendant's actions were so grievous as to warrant punishment.)

"We have not done the job to make this as friendly a workplace as it should be for females," said Reed V. Hillman, the superintendent of the Massachusetts State Police. "We have made mistakes."[16]

Often, however, it has been found that when a policewoman suffers some harm from a fellow officer or the police department at large, such as sexual harassment, gender bias, discriminatory rules, and so on, and she complains about it, the policewoman quickly suffers retaliation, sometimes from other officers and sometimes from the police department administration. A number of policewomen have had to resort to lawsuits in order to fight this type of retaliation.

In 2005, for example, Detective Sergeant Ya-May Christie of the Los Angeles Police Department filed a complaint against her boss, Internal Affairs Deputy Chief Michael Berkow. She alleged in her complaint that Berkow gave special treatment, including coveted positions, to policewomen who had sex with him. Christie also alleged that Berkow attempted to influence a case she was investigating that involved a policewoman who reportedly had had sex with him. Following her filing of this complaint, Christie said she began experiencing retaliation, including a demotion and transfer. As a result, Christie sued.

In October 2007 a jury found in Christie's favor. They awarded her more than $1 million in damages. "Hopefully this sends a message to the city that they have a problem and that they have to fix it," said Christie's lawyer, Bradley C. Gage.[17]

It isn't only policewomen, however, who can be retaliated against when it comes to sexual harassment complaints. Lieutenant Diane Mancini of the Teaneck, New Jersey, Police Department sued the department in 2000 for sexual harassment and for retaliation from the department for complaining about the sexual harassment. A jury in June 2000 awarded her $1.1 million, which included $500,000 in punitive damages. Police officer John Shouldis testified in Lieutenant Mancini's favor during her trial. Following this, according to court testimony, members of the police department denied Shouldis a promotion, took away his overtime, watched him every day as he signed in and out, and threatened him with expulsion from the police union.

Shouldis sued the police department, and in June 2008 a jury found in his favor. They awarded him $4.1 million, which included $1.5 million in punitive damages. In April 2009, the Township Council voted to pay the judgment rather than try to appeal it. "I think it's fair to say we're trying to learn from our experiences," said Teaneck Mayor Kevie Feit.[18]

Sadly, sometimes even organizations that are supposed to protect police officers can turn against them in sexual harassment cases. In 1998, Officer Vanessa Dixon of the Lowell, Massachusetts, Police Department went on a trip sponsored by her union, the International Brotherhood of Police Officers. During the bus ride, the other police officers on the bus (Vanessa was the only policewoman on the bus) allegedly made numerous sexual and threatening comments to her. Although the president of the union also rode on the bus, he reportedly made no effort to stop the harassment.

Even though Dixon didn't report the incident, the police department found out about it and began an investigation. The union president went on television, and, in Dixon's words, disparaged her. She sued for discrimination, retaliation, and defamation. A court found in her favor and awarded her $2.2 million, including $1 million in punitive damages.

Because of the cases we've talked about and many others, a number of police departments, after themselves paying out or witnessing other police departments pay out huge sums of money over sexual harassment claims, have initiated policies that can protect them from such claims. For example, many police departments have now adopted strict anti-sexual harassment policies, in which support for the policy comes from the top brass, and everyone on the police department receives training concerning what sexual harassment is and what steps should be taken if it arises.

The sexual harassment policy of a police department, if it is to be effective, must be detailed and clear about what constitutes sexual harassment. The policy must also make clear the complaint procedure to follow for violations, including the right to skip the chain of command if the next person in line is the perpetrator. Under an effective sexual harassment policy, action is taken by the police department immediately upon receipt of a complaint. Although such a policy may not prevent a lawsuit, it can be a strong defense that limits a police department's liability.

In other areas, also in order to protect themselves against expensive lawsuits, many police departments have restructured their entry and promotional systems and also their policies concerning pregnancy. These police departments have examined their policies in these areas to make sure there is no intentional or unintentional bias against women.

Putting policies such as these in place can be crucial not only for the fiscal welfare of the police department, but also for the welfare of the careers of top police officials. For example, in February 2009 a jury found in favor of New Jersey Transit Police Lieutenant Theresa Frizalone. She sued for sexual harassment and for retaliation when she complained about the sexual harassment. The jury awarded her $1,449,000, which included $1 million in punitive damages. Within twenty-four hours of the jury's verdict, the chief of the New Jersey Transit Police was gone and a new chief was in his place.

Of course, as we've talked about several times in other chapters, prejudicial behavior against policewomen isn't limited to just the United States. In 2006, a court in Canada awarded Royal Canadian Mounted Police Officer Nancy Schultz $950,000. They found that her supervisor began harassing her soon after she reported she was pregnant.

Policewomen, as we have seen so far in this book, have faced many obstacles in their quest to gain entry into police departments and then advance within them, even though example after example across the country has demonstrated the huge benefit to police departments of hiring women. Some police departments, however, regardless of the mounting evidence of the value of policewomen, have attempted to erect obstacles, such as physical agility tests and biased promotional exams, in an attempt to derail the movement of women into and within law enforcement. Yet, as we will see in the next chapter, many women have nevertheless still managed to get onto these police departments and advance upward through the organizations to hold ranks and positions unheard of before 1968.

**7**

# POLICEWOMEN AFTER CAR 47

In September 1964 twenty-two-year-old Penny Harrington joined the Portland, Oregon, Police Department. During her first eight years with the department she followed a path similar to most female police officers of the time. She worked in the Juvenile Branch and in Planning and Research.

Then, in January 1972, she became a detective and began working burglaries, fraud, and sex crimes. Her first real step upward in the Portland Police Department chain of command came in July 1972 when the department promoted her to the rank of sergeant. In February 1977 the Portland Police Department promoted her again, this time to the rank of lieutenant, after which she became a precinct shift commander.

Harrington's rise seemed unstoppable, and indeed it was. In July 1980 the Portland Police Department promoted her to the rank of captain. At this rank she served as both the personnel director and a precinct commander.

Then, in January 1985, all of Penny Harrington's hard work paid off. An event unheard of in a major American city occurred. The newly elected mayor of Portland appointed Penny Harrington, a woman, to be the new chief of police.

Although Chief Harrington's rise within the Portland Police Department may have looked to outsiders to be easy and seamless, it was anything but. During her career she had to constantly fight for her right to be treated equally with the men in the department. During her career, she filed over forty sex discrimination lawsuits against the Portland Police Department. But most important, she kept winning them and moving up in rank.

Penny Harrington, however, didn't land in an easy job when she became the chief of police. She came into office at a time when crime had reached an all-time high in Portland. The city ranked eighth in violent crimes out of the 183 cities in the United States with populations of more than 100,000. And it ranked sixth in property crimes.

And, as if this wasn't already a tough enough place, Harrington quickly realized that her every move and action as chief of police would be watched, and that the likelihood of future female police chiefs in other cities rested almost entirely on her actions. She knew that politicians and police administrators all across the country were going to be keeping close tabs on her, and that any slip-up she made would be broadcast far and wide.

Since Penny Harrington was the first woman in the United States to be named chief of police of a major city, naturally dozens of members of the media swarmed to Portland to interview her and constantly shadow her every action in office. She appeared on *Good Morning, America, The Merv Griffin Show, The NBC Nightly News,* and other national television media outlets. In addition, articles about her appeared in *People, USA Today,* the *New York Times,* and many other publications.

However, along with the pressure of the ever-present news media and the knowledge that her every action was being scrutinized, soon after taking office as chief of police, Harrington ran afoul of the local police union because of her actions following an accidental death. A Portland police officer accidentally killed a black security guard while using a carotid choke hold that is supposed to only render a person unconscious. Naturally, the community was alarmed and outraged by the death, but then following the tragedy several police officers did something totally outrageous that really inflamed the community.

The day of the security guard's funeral, several Portland police officers stood in the parking lot of a police department station house selling

T-shirts that said, "Don't choke 'em. Smoke 'em." Under the words was the picture of a smoking gun. This callous behavior, of course, brought a firestorm of criticism. "This is what you would expect from police hit squads in El Salvador," said Ron Herndon, co-chairman of the Black United Front.[1]

One of Chief Harrington's main goals when she took over the Portland Police Department was to improve the department's image with the community. She knew that this unbelievably insensitive act could easily set that goal back many years. As chief of police, she had to deal with this situation, and do it in a way so that the public could see there was no cover-up, as she did during her entire administration. "We don't have anything to hide," Chief Harrington once told a reporter for the *New York Times*, "so there's no need to stonewall the public."[2]

Consequently, Chief Harrington, naturally very upset by her officers' incredible act of insensitivity, called the officers in and fired them. The local police union president tried to dissuade her, but she wouldn't relent. And because she wouldn't, from that day forward the union and many of Portland's police officers opposed her at every step. Every program she initiated and every new idea she attempted was scrutinized and criticized.

Although this opposition to Chief Harrington from within the Portland Police Department may have seemed, and indeed was, extreme, I don't believe it happened simply because she was a woman. The very same thing has happened to many male chiefs of police.

Police work can at times be a very dangerous occupation, and in order to survive officers realize that they have to depend on each other for their safety. Officers know from experience that they can't always depend on the public for help, and so they must depend on each other. This mutual need for each other usually results in an extremely tight emotional bond forming between the officers. Consequently, most officer-level members of a police department feel that other similar ranking members are part of their extended family, and consequently they take very personally any attack on a family member or members, including what they see as attacks from high-ranking officers. And because police officers are so protective of each other, unless an act committed by one of them is totally corrupt and unworthy, they will usually stand behind officers who are disciplined, in opposition to the chief and command staff, who they more often than not see as being out of touch and uncaring about the plight of ordinary police officers.

For six years I served as Executive Officer of the Indianapolis Police Department, and part of that job included meting out discipline. I can recall only a time or two in those six years when the body of the police department supported me in the discipline I handed out, even though the officers receiving the discipline during those years had had many chances before they came to my attention, and more than deserved the discipline I gave them. Even my own family members on the police department didn't support or understand much of the discipline I handed out, often saying they thought I was just being a "butthole."

To make matters worse, in times of stress, many police officers, rather than reaching out to the public for support, instead close ranks and isolate themselves. This is why the union and other Portland police officers were so vehemently opposed to firing the officers selling the T-shirts. They were a tightly bound family who saw themselves as being persecuted by both the public and the police department command staff.

So my point here is that the adversarial relationship Chief Harrington found herself in with the police union and members of the Portland Police Department had nothing to do with her gender. It has happened to many, many male chiefs of police.

Penny Harrington's legacy, however, doesn't have anything to do with the turmoil of her tenure as chief, but rather, like Liz and Betty's legacy in Car 47, her legacy in Portland was that she opened doors previously closed to women. Following Penny Harrington's tenure as chief of the Portland Police Department: in 1990 Houston appointed Elizabeth Watson as chief of police; in 1994 Atlanta named Beverly Harvard as their chief of police; in 1995 Montgomery County, Maryland, appointed Carol Mehrling as the new chief of police; in 2000 Jan Strauss became chief of the Mesa, Arizona, Police Department; and in 2003, Ella Bully-Cummings took over as the chief of police of Detroit, while in the same year Julia Grimes took over the reins as the Director of the Alaska State Police.

≫

Although Penny Harrington's rise to chief of police of a major American city only seventeen years after Liz and Betty rolled out in Car 47 might appear to some readers as a radical change in the mentality of American police departments regarding the value of policewomen, the mentality really hadn't changed that much in most other police departments by 1985, and unfortunately it still hasn't changed that much today in many police departments. The women chiefs of police cited previously are the exception rather than the rule. Many police departments even today, almost a decade into the twenty-first century, still attempt to discourage women from applying to become police officers. One of the most common ways they do this is by requiring female applicants to pass physical agility tests with standards set for men.

From my experience as a police officer for almost forty years, I do believe that anyone who wants to be a law enforcement officer must possess the strength necessary to do the job, which includes enough strength to restrain ordinary people, force open doors, chase fleeing individuals, and other such tasks. But a law enforcement officer doesn't have to be a body builder. Rather, a good police officer should possess average strength and above-average common sense. As a matter of fact, sometimes having the strength of a body builder would not help at all, but could actually be detrimental. As the following anecdote demonstrates, even though physically fit, a good police officer must know his or her strengths and limitations, and not get involved in situations that he or she can't handle alone.

≫

Once, when I was a uniformed street officer, the police department received an emergency call from a distraught mother who told the dispatcher in gasping breaths that her son had suddenly gone berserk and was tearing up her house. She and her husband, she told the dispatcher from a neighbor's phone, had raced out of the house to escape his rampage. The dispatcher gave the run to me and another officer. As it turned out, I was only a block or two from the address and arrived there very quickly. Stepping out of my car, I spotted a disheveled man and woman standing in the driveway of the address I'd been given. I walked up to them and asked what the problem was.

"It's our son Arnold," the woman told me, her breath still coming in small gasps. "We had all just sat down to dinner and all of a sudden he went crazy and started tearing up the house."

"Does he have any weapons?" I asked her.

She shook her head. "He's just using his hands. I think he's having some kind of flashback to Vietnam because he kept calling us 'VC bastards.'"

I nodded and then walked back to the police car and used the radio to ask the dispatcher how close my backup was. The dispatcher responded a few moments later that the officer was still several minutes away. Thanking him, I decided to have a look inside the house to see if perhaps I could settle this situation myself. I had had several cases like this before in which people had suddenly become violent and then damaged property, and I knew that often these people would quiet down a few minutes after the initial rage. I started walking toward the house.

"Officer!" the woman called in a shrill, alarmed voice, the tone of which caused me to stop and look back at her. "You should probably know that he's a Marine karate instructor at Parris Island."

At that moment I heard what sounded like a man screaming, followed by the sound of breaking furniture and smashing glass. Did I show my bravery and manhood and go on into the house anyway?

No, I didn't. Instead, I got on the radio and told the dispatcher what I had and asked him for several more cars as backups. Then I waited outside with the parents for them to arrive.

Eventually, when we had half a dozen police officers there, plus an ambulance to take the man to the county hospital mental ward, we shouted through the front door and were finally able to talk Arnold out of the house and into the front yard. He stayed in a karate readiness position the whole time as he stalked around the yard, calling us "VC bastards" over and over.

Several minutes passed as Arnold moved carefully around the yard, always staying in a readiness position and never letting any of us get behind him. Then, all at once, he gave a spinning kick at a nearby tree and snapped off a large limb four or five feet off the ground. We were in a quandary. Unless he attacked one of us, we couldn't just shoot him, particularly with his parents standing right there, and to try to grab him while he was in a combat readiness position would have been incredibly stupid. And so, for a time that seemed much longer than it probably was, we stood and watched as Arnold practiced karate kicks and mumbled mostly to himself. Finally, after several tense minutes, and for some unknown reason, Arnold suddenly clasped his hands to his face and fell to the ground sobbing. We instantly swooped on him, and it took every officer there to restrain him so that he couldn't hurt anyone while we fastened him with belts to a stretcher.

≪

The point of this anecdote is that no police officer, no matter how fit, strong, or in shape, can handle every situation without help. If I had been a body builder type and had possessed huge amounts of strength, would I have gone on into the house by myself? I might have, and very likely would have been seriously injured or perhaps even killed. But I didn't. Instead, we used common sense and a group effort. Therefore, my point is that everyone who becomes a police officer doesn't have to have huge, bulging muscles to be effective.

Consequently, for police departments to expect female police applicants to be in shape and possess average strength is reasonable, but to expect them to be as strong as men is both ridiculous and unreasonable. On average, women have only about 60 percent of the upper body strength of men. This is simply a physiological rule of nature. Yet still, many police departments require female candidates to compete in upper body strength testing on an equal basis with men. This doesn't make any sense, but then it often doesn't have to because physical agility testing is many times not really a test, but simply a ruse to keep women from successfully applying to become police officers. "For years, police agencies have systematically kept women away, mainly by using agility tests that focus on upper-body strength," said Katherine Spillar, executive vice president of the Feminist Majority.[3]

I recently checked the websites of police departments in several dozen cities across the United States and found that almost all of them have a physical agility test, usually scored as pass/fail, which measures for upper body strength. Although this is not bad in itself, what is bad is that in many of the police departments men and women applicants compete equally, and must demonstrate the same amount of upper body strength, regardless of the natural differences between men and women.

At the websites I checked, I found that some police departments do this upper body strength testing by requiring the applicants to complete a certain number of push-ups in a specified time. Others test it by requiring candidates to scale a six-foot solid wall, and some require applicants to push heavy objects or drag weighted dummies.

My wife, who worked as a police officer for twenty-four years, had to pass a physical agility test at the Indianapolis Police Department that included scaling a six-foot solid wall. Whereas men can often use their upper body strength to pull themselves up and over the wall, only a small number of women can do it this way. The secret for individuals without a lot of upper body strength is to swing one of their legs over the top of the wall, and then use the strength of their legs and lower body (which is closer to equal in men and women) to pull the rest of their body over the wall. My wife, in order to pass this segment of the physical agility test, practiced for several weeks in order to master this technique. Unfortunately, although this may work for solid wall climbs, other tests such as push-ups, dummy drags, and so on are harder to master without a lot of upper body strength, and will usually eliminate a large number of women applicants.

Although many police departments use physical agility tests as a ruse to selectively eliminate many female candidates, not all police departments want their physical agility test to purposely flunk out women. The Sacramento, California, Police Department, for instance, sponsors a "female fitness challenge" to assist women who want to pass their physical agility test. According to an article in the magazine *Law and Order,* "In addition to providing female candidates with an opportunity to develop the requisite skills needed to successfully pass the physical agility test, the fitness challenge enables female candidates to work with a personal trainer once a week over a three-month period to improve their overall physical condition."[4] Unfortunately, however, Sacramento is more the exception than the rule.

Therefore, as might be expected, because police department physical agility tests are so often set up with the intention of eliminating a much higher number of women than men, the courts have often thrown them out when they have been challenged. One of the most recent legal challenges is that of a number of women who couldn't pass the Eire, Pennsylvania, Police Department physical agility test.

In December 2005, U.S. District Court Judge Sean J. McLaughlin ruled that the Eire Police Department had violated federal law under

Title VII of the Civil Rights Act of 1964 in its use of a physical agility test that disproportionately disqualified women. Eighty-seven percent of women versus only 29 percent of men failed the Eire Police Department physical agility test. The court also looked at the fact that Eire had been using the test since 1994, and that, by 2005, only 4 percent of its police force were women, which is far below the national average.

Eire's physical agility test consisted of an obstacle course, followed by a series of push-ups and sit-ups within a ninety-second period. The court said it could find no valid reason for the inclusion of the push-ups and sit-ups, or the ninety-second cutoff. Wan J. Kim, assistant attorney general for the Civil Rights Division of the Department of Justice, stated:

> Title VII and common sense allow public safety employers to use tests that validly measure an applicant's ability to do the job. But it is unlawful to use tests that wrongly disqualify applicants who otherwise could perform the job's important public safety mission. We are pleased that the court recognized the inequities in Eire's test.[5]

In March 2006 the city of Eire, in response to the court's decision, entered into a consent decree with the U.S. government. Under the decree, the Eire Police Department had to make offers of employment to female applicants who had been denied employment solely because of the physical agility test, and also give them back pay and retroactive seniority. The city of Eire additionally agreed not to use any more tests that had a disparate effect on female applicants.

Interestingly, some physical agility tests, like Eire's with their push-ups and sit-ups, ask candidates to do things that no police officer has to do or would do. As another example, the California Highway Patrol, in its physical agility testing in the early 1990s, required applicants to scale two walls. One was four feet, ten inches high, and the other was six feet high. The candidates then had to simulate handcuffing someone, and afterward return over both walls to the police car. The handcuffing simulation consisted of manipulating an "arrest resistor device," which involved pulling together and holding two mechanical arms exerting forty pounds of resistance on the left and sixty-five pounds of resistance on the right.

In reality, however, as any experienced police officer will tell you, no one person, no matter how strong, can by him or herself successfully handcuff another person who doesn't want to be handcuffed, short of beating the person senseless first. It simply can't be done without seriously hurting the person being handcuffed. And as for going back over the walls after successfully simulating the handcuffing, no real police officer would ever do this. What would stop the handcuffed person you left behind from just getting up and running away? Instead, a real police officer would wait with the prisoner and call for backup. The requirements of this unrealistic simulation used as a physical agility test disqualified many women, which made it ripe for a challenge.

In the case *Dothard v. Rawlinson,* which we discussed in the previous chapter, the court stated, "To establish a prima facie case of discrimination, a plaintiff need only show that the facially neutral standards in question select applicants for hire in a significantly discriminating pattern."[6] If a plaintiff, therefore, can show that this is so, then the burden of proof shifts to the testing agency, which must prove to the court that the test used, even though discriminatory, is nevertheless a valid measure of some quality crucial to doing the job. But, as often has been found, this can many times be very difficult for police departments to do.

As a matter of fact, another case involving a police department and physical agility testing very clearly demonstrates the difficulty of doing this. In the case of *Thomas v. City of Evanston,* several women who couldn't pass the physical agility test required to become an Evanston, Illinois, police officer filed a lawsuit challenging the test. The police department, however, claimed that it had developed the test using a job analysis of the tasks required of police officers in various Illinois cities. The court, in throwing out the test, stated, "Too often tests which on the surface appear objective and scientific turn out to be based on ingrained stereotypes and speculative assumptions about what is 'necessary' to do the job."[7]

According to Equal Employment Opportunity Commission standards, if the number of women who can pass a test is less than 80 percent of the number of men who can pass a test, the police department must then show that the test measures an ability that is an essential requirement of the job. In addition, the police department must also show that the test being used is the least discriminatory measure available.

As a paper in the journal *Public Personnel Management* stated, "It is certainly reasonable to assert that physical agility and stamina are rationally related to required on-the-job behaviors of police officers. However, there is an enormous gap between making that assertion and upholding a particular set of physical selection standards." The article then goes on to state, "It is not an overstatement to say that no other aspect of the personnel selection process is fraught with more difficulty or clouded with more ambiguity than physical ability testing."[8] Also discussing this point, another paper in *Public Personnel Management* stated, "Physical ability tests (which are associated with a relatively high litigation rate) did not fare as well in terms of case outcome. Physical ability tests survived only 58 percent of challenges brought against them."[9]

The reason for this low level of success is because a number of the courts that have ruled on lawsuits challenging physical agility tests have stated that the tests used must, as discussed previously, closely resemble the tasks a person performing the job would be required to do. This is easy for some public safety jobs, such as firefighting, in which the physical agility tests often involve the applicants dragging fire hoses, climbing ladders, dragging body-size and weighted dummies a certain distance, and so on. It is easy because these are tasks that firefighters do on a regular basis.

Most police work, on the other hand, is not that clear-cut. Most uniformed police work involves riding in a police car and waiting for radio runs. And although some runs may involve physical exertion, including chasing and wrestling with suspects, the majority of runs don't. The majority usually involve talking to people in order to extract a bit of the information needed to solve a case, following leads on other people to talk to, who may or may not give the officer more bits of information, and then finally writing up a report when all the information available has been obtained. And although many police departments, including Indianapolis, use a six-foot solid wall climb as part of their physical agility test, never in thirty-eight years did I ever have to scale a six-foot solid wall. The same can be said for push-ups and sit-ups. Unlike firefighters, whose job is regularly strenuous, only occasionally do police officers become involved in strenuous physical tasks.

Police work has been described as "ninety-nine percent boredom broken by one percent of stark terror." This is a very accurate description because police officers can often go days, weeks, or even months without doing anything strenuous at all, and then suddenly become involved in a long foot chase followed by a life-and-death struggle with a suspect. Unlike firefighting, in police work there are simply no regular day-to-day physical activities to use as measurements for physical agility tests. Special Agent John Gales Sauls, a legal instructor at the FBI Academy, said,

> Abstract measures of fitness, such as push-ups, which do not obviously replicate on-the-job tasks, are generally found by courts not to be a product of business necessity. Unfortunately for law enforcement managers, the physical tasks of a police officer are not as obvious as those of a firefighter and neither are they as broadly related to successful job performance.[10]

In 2003, a survey of sixty-two police agencies in the United States by the National Center for Women & Policing found that 89 percent of them (fifty-five agencies) had physical agility tests (100 percent of the state agencies surveyed, 94.7 percent of the city agencies, and 76.2 percent of the county agencies). The survey discovered that 89 percent of the agencies scored the tests on a pass/fail basis, and that the fifty-five agencies used many different tests, including obstacle courses, running tracks, solid-wall climbs, push-ups, sit-ups, weighted dummy drags, and other measures of physical strength and stamina. But even for those police departments that used the same type of tests, there were no consistent standards for the pass/fail cutoff; each department's measure for success and failure was different. More important, however, only 27.3 percent of the agencies used gender norming for their scoring, and only 25.5 percent used age norming. For the remaining agencies, all applicants, men and women, young and old, had to match the same standards.[11]

As we talked about previously, the overriding problem with police work and physical agility testing, which often becomes the basis of many lawsuits challenging these tests, is that there are no real benchmarks for physical performance. For example, as part of a physical agility test a police applicant might have to run a half mile or longer. But how fast should this be done? Some fleeing suspects can be fast and agile, whereas others can be slow and ponderous. So what standards should police departments use? No one is sure. As another example, some police departments require applicants to do a certain number of push-ups. But, unlike firefighting, which has clear, job-related tasks such as dragging hose or climbing ladders, no police officer is ever required to do push-ups, so how can a benchmark for these be set?

The answer is that it can't, which makes many police departments' physical agility tests murky measurements at best. Consequently, when applicants challenge these tests in court, police departments often have a difficult time justifying their requirements.

And, of course, an interesting and relevant point many police departments overlook in developing physical agility tests is that many of their present officers, who are performing their jobs at successful levels, couldn't pass the physical agility test required of applicants. We discovered this problem at the Indianapolis Police Department when we attempted to establish a baseline for minimum physical standards for our officers. Many of our officers, we found, including a number of high-ranking ones, couldn't meet the minimum standards, even though at the time they were successfully performing their jobs. We consequently abandoned the idea.

In the case of *Lanning v. Southeastern Pennsylvania Transit Authority*, the court held that employers who use physical agility tests that have an adverse impact must not only demonstrate that the trait or ability being measured is important to the job, but that the passing score is set at the minimum amount of ability needed to do the job. In other words, if current police officers who are successfully doing their jobs cannot pass the test, the passing score is set too high and is unlawful.[12]

To solve the many problems caused by physical agility testing, a number of experts now recommend health-based screening for police applicants rather than physical agility testing. This health-based screening measures an applicant's health and fitness, and is normed for the applicant's age and sex, thereby eliminating any claims of discrimination. Then, following graduation from the training academy and completion of its often strenuous physical instruction, applicants can be tested for the physical agility measures shown as being necessary to be effective police officers.

Many police departments have discovered, to their dismay, however, that physical agility tests can turn out to be double-edged swords. On the one hand, police departments can be accused of using these tests to discriminate against women, but on the other hand, they can also face serious liability issues if they don't ensure that their recruits meet at least some physical standards. For example, not doing any physical testing at all can lead to lawsuits for "negligent hiring" in which plaintiffs make the claim that a police department hired a person it knew, or should have known, wasn't capable of performing the job, and that consequently the plaintiff or someone else was injured. The goal for police departments, therefore, is to develop a system that allows them to disqualify candidates who can't do the job, without at the same time discriminating against women. The way to reach this goal is through the health-based screening described previously.

To wrap up our discussion of physical agility testing, I quote from a paper published by the National Center for Women & Policing:

> In fact, there are no documented cases of negative outcomes due to a lack of strength or aggression exhibited by a female officer. Research documents that police officers are not generally killed in the line of duty because of physical weakness but "due to circumstances beyond their control, or as a result of poor judgment." Physical strength does not play a primary role in these tragedies, nor does it explain why men are disproportionately more likely than women to be killed in the line of duty.[13]

And for any detractors who claim that they can find a case in which the lack of strength or aggression by a female officer did lead to bad consequences, I'd counter by saying that in my own experience I can tell a number of stories about male officers who got into trouble because of a lack of strength or aggression.

Physical agility tests, however, aren't the only method some police departments use in their attempt to discourage women from applying to become police officers. Some police departments have also been known to use interview boards set up with the intention of finding reasons to reject women. Chief Carol Sletner told me:

I recall a police department interview that I went to. When I walked in, one of the officers on the panel actually said out loud to his colleagues, "Oh-oh, a woman." Suffice to say, I knew I wouldn't get a callback from that particular agency. In fact, once I left the interview I then had to go and take the physical agility test. I came very close to just skipping the test, but then changed my mind. I've never been a quitter, so I went through with the test and passed it. Later, I got a letter from the department stating I didn't score high enough to get a spot on their hiring list.[14]

Yet, despite the efforts of many police department's to keep women off of the force through physical agility tests, biased interview boards, and so on, the percentage of policewomen across the nation began to grow after Liz and Betty's breakthrough in 1968. In 1972 in a survey of cities with populations of 250,000 or more, researchers found that only 2 percent of the police officers were women. In 1978, this had grown to 4.2 percent, and to 8.8 percent by 1986.[15] In 1987, of all police departments nationally, regardless of city size, women made up 7.6 percent of the officers, 8.1 percent in 1990, and 8.8 percent in 1993.[16] By 2000, the number of policewomen nationally had risen to 13 percent.[17]

However, these numbers are just overall averages, and, as might be expected, different types of agencies have acquired different numbers of female officers. For example, it wasn't until 1972 that the Pennsylvania State Police became the first state police agency in the United States to hire women for road patrol. Consequently, state police agencies are still trying to catch up. In 2003, of the 57,000 state troopers nationally, only 6.7 percent were women.[18] And yet even this number is not spread evenly. A newspaper article published in January 2009 stated that of West Virginia's 656 state troopers, only 17, or 2.6 percent, were women.[19]

On the other hand, as of June 2002, 14.8 percent of all federal law enforcement officers were women. Like the state police agencies, the Secret Service and the FBI didn't hire their first female agents until 1972. And even though prior to 1972 the FBI had no female agents, by 2002, 18 percent of the FBI's agents were women.[20]

Regardless of how much progress has been made in increasing the number of policewomen nationally over the last forty or so years, some police departments, particularly small ones, have nevertheless refused to grow with the times. Even almost a decade into the twenty-first century many small police departments either haven't hired any women yet or are just beginning to hire them.

For example, in July 2000, South River, New Jersey, with a police force of thirty-two officers, hired its first-ever female officer. "History was made today in the first female officer," said Chief of Police Wesley Bomba.[21]

In June 2001 Pelham, Massachusetts, a town that has been in existence since 1739, employed its first female officer. "Her credentials are just amazing," said Chief of Police Evan Haglund.[22]

In July 2004, thirty-six years after Liz and Betty rolled out in Car 47, Edison, New Jersey, with a population of more than 100,000 people, announced that it was bringing on a third female officer to complement its department of 206 men and 2 women.

The city of Malverne, New York, in July 2007 hired its first female officer. "It's a big deal because, for 80 years, people have always seen male police officers," said Malverne Police Chief John Aresta. "It's something they're not used to seeing."[23]

The police department of the city of Putnam, Connecticut, reportedly dates back 112 years. Still, it wasn't until December 2008 that the department employed its first female officer.

Unfortunately, however, the small police agencies mentioned here are still in the minority. Thousands of small police agencies nationally have yet to hire their first female officer. But despite the stubbornness of these holdouts, the number of policewomen being hired across the United States continued to grow after 1968, from less than 2 percent nationally until the number reached double-digit percentage numbers. And along with these increasing numbers of policewomen came many stories of success, of women who, against stern opposition, nevertheless achieved goals unattainable before 1968.

For example, following Officer Donna Holmes' completion of the training academy in 1968, the Indianapolis Police Department assigned her to be the secretary of the Homicide Branch. However, after Liz and Betty broke the street patrol barrier, other barriers also began coming down. Donna Holmes eventually returned to the Homicide Branch, but this time as a homicide detective, something unheard of before in the Indianapolis Police Department.

"I probably wanted to be a detective in homicide more than anything in my life," said Detective Holmes. "Not only to be a detective here but the first woman detective makes me feel special. I'm glad they've given me the opportunity to show them a woman can do it."[24]

When I assumed command of the Indianapolis Police Department Homicide Branch a number of years later in 1999, there were several female detectives already there. Soon after my arrival, the department promoted one of these detectives to sergeant, and I made her a unit leader. Also, no one had much concern about it when I later brought in a female section leader (lieutenant). In addition, whenever we held interviews for new detectives, no one on the selection board gave any thought at all to whether the candidate was male or female.

As discussed in chapter 5, Columbia County, Georgia, Sheriff's Deputy Judy Thomason, despite considerable opposition from the men, became her department's first female canine officer. Although many of the men may have opposed this move, the Sheriff's Department administration obviously disagreed with them. "We think it's very important for our agency to mirror the community in which we serve," said Sheriff's Captain Steve Morris about Deputy Thomason's assignment.[25]

In Janesville, Wisconsin, in 1998 Officer Laura Hauser became a hostage negotiator. This is a highly sought-after position in police departments that comes with tremendous responsibility. Hostage negotiators must interact with highly agitated hostage-takers, attempt to calm them down, and try to work out a peaceful solution to the hostage situation. In my book *SWAT Teams*,[26] I discuss how more hostage incidents are resolved by hostage negotiators than through any other method. But, in addition to her prestigious new assignment, Officer Hauser in 2007 also received the Mary Rita Ostrander Leadership Award, the highest award for a police officer in Wisconsin.

As more examples of policewomen moving into previously male-only jobs, several police departments in 2006 through 2008 reported assigning policewomen to their motorcycle units, another often-coveted position. These police departments include Pittsburgh, Pennsylvania; Lexington, Kentucky; and Wayne County (Detroit), Michigan.

An even more impressive advancement was achieved by Officer Jessica Lessuise of the Northville, Michigan, Police Department. In 2006 she graduated from the Western Wayne County Special Operations

Team program, and consequently landed a position on her department's SWAT team. "I like the team aspect of SWAT and the top-notch training," Jessica said.[27]

Yet, despite Officer Lessuise's prestigious assignment, a study completed in 1992 found that, although female officers made up 10 percent of all police officers nationally, only 1 percent of the members of the police tactical squads (SWAT) were women. Police administrators were asked by researchers why so few women belonged to tactical units: "Among the explanations offered by the respondents in this study included the lack of seniority needed to apply for a position in a tactical unit, the lack of military experience, the irregular hours, and the demanding physical standards required for selection and continued assignment."[28]

Although being part of a tactical unit does require more strength and stamina than being an ordinary police officer, the fact that 1 percent of the units are women shows that women can make the grade if only given a fair chance. As a matter of fact, according to the study cited previously,

> The responding supervisory personnel felt that in some cases female officers possess inherent characteristics that are actually a distinct advantage in tactical operations. For example, a smaller physical stature has allowed some female officers to be especially adept at window entry under stealth conditions and other activities conducted in cramped quarters requiring agility and flexibility.[29]

Finally, another previously male-only assignment that policewomen have gained entry into is vice work. Although at one time many police departments strictly prohibited policewomen from working vice, many police supervisors today have found that some vice assignments are much easier to complete if they use female detectives, that some locations are easier for women to access, and that some jobs such as prostitution stings can only be accomplished by women.

When I was a field captain on the west side of Indianapolis, we often received complaints from residents about prostitutes and their "johns" (customers) congregating in their neighborhoods. To combat this problem, we detailed female officers to pose as prostitutes and then arrested the men attempting to patronize them. During these prostitution stings, we often arrested so many men that we had to pull the policewomen off of the detail because of the backlog in processing the arrested men. But most important, word would quickly get around about the arrests, and the johns would no longer frequent the area, forcing the prostitutes to move.

Some policewomen after 1968, in addition to moving into previously male-only assignments, also began moving up in rank; a small number of them reaching command level. According to the April 1975 issue of *Ladies Home Journal*, by 1975 twenty-eight large cities had assigned policewomen to street patrol. But, in addition, by this time there was already a female captain in Philadelphia, female inspectors in New York City and Detroit, and a female deputy chief of traffic in Chicago.[30]

As another example, in 1975, the Honolulu Police Department had only fifteen women on its force of 1,500 officers. By 2004, the number had grown to 149, with one female major, one captain, five lieutenants, fifteen sergeants, and seventeen detectives.

Although I talked earlier in this chapter about a number of women who have become chiefs of police, a number of other policewomen have also worked their way up to command-level rank. For example, when Joan Yale joined the Nassau County, New York, Police Department in 1974, she faced considerable opposition from the male officers because she was the first policewoman to be hired by Nassau County. However, she stuck it out. By September 2006, she had been a sergeant, lieutenant, captain, inspector, chief of patrol, and finally chief of detectives.

Another example is Karin Montejo, who retired after spending thirty years at the Miami-Dade Police Department. During her time there she held such ranks and positions as captain of the Economic Crimes Bureau, major of the Domestic Crimes Bureau, major of the Sexual Crimes Bureau, district commander, and division chief for the Administration and Technology Division.

Along with these women who have attained command-level ranks in municipal police departments, in November 1992, Jacquelyn H. Barrett, of Fulton County, Georgia, became the country's first elected black female sheriff. With twenty years of law enforcement experience, Barrett was so well liked by the members of the deputies' union that they put up her $2,184 qualifying fee so that she could run for the office of sheriff. "There have been occasions when you know that you were kept back just because of your gender, and that was difficult," said Barrett. "But you stick with it and you go on."[31]

On the federal level, in 2002 Kathleen Kiernan, after twenty years with the Bureau of Alcohol, Tobacco, and Firearms (ATF), became an Assistant Director in Washington, D.C. "There is no 'typical day' at the office, which makes the job and career so exciting," said Kiernan.[32] Along with her high rank, Kiernan also established a number of other "firsts" at ATF: the first female explosives-expert instructor, the first female member of the National Response Team, and the first female graduate of the Redstone Hazardous Devices School.

Finally, in 2005 Chief of Police Mary Ann Viverette of the Gaithersburg, Maryland, Police Department became the president of the International Association of Chiefs of Police. This is the oldest, largest, and most prestigious law enforcement organization in the world. It presently has more than 20,000 members in more than one hundred countries. Readers will recall that in chapter 2 we talked about how this organization nearly threw out Officer Alice Stebbins Wells when she attempted to address them in 1914.

Although the movement of policewomen into all ranks and areas of the nation's police departments was certainly a victory in the fight for equality with men, this victory nevertheless had a serious downside to it. As we will see in the next chapter, being a successful policewoman, no matter what rank or assignment, can often cause a severe strain in the emotional relationships a woman has with her husband, parents, children, and anyone else she may be emotionally involved with.

## 8

# STRAIN ON RELATIONSHIPS

Michele Hashem Schlindwein was born into a police family. Her father, Al Hashem, served on the Boston Police Department for thirty years before retiring when Michele was ten years old. Following her father's retirement, Michele and her family moved to North Port, Florida, a little community about thirty-five miles southeast of Sarasota, where Al opened a restaurant. People who knew her in North Port remembered Michele as a happy, outgoing girl.

After high school, Michele met German-born Peter Schlindwein and fell in love. The two married and moved to Germany, where Michele gave birth to a son, Christopher. However, after less than a year in Germany, they moved back to Florida and Michele took a job as a dispatcher at the North Port Police Department.

Michele never told anyone, including her family members, but her real desire was to become a police officer like her father. Consequently, she enrolled in the Sarasota Police Academy without telling anyone. Her father, invited on a ruse to the Sarasota Training Academy Graduation Dinner, sat stunned when he heard his daughter's name being called as a graduate of the academy. Tears showed his pride when she presented him with a class photo that she had signed, "To my Pop, the Cop."[1]

In 1979, following Michele's graduation, the North Port Police Department swore her in as their first female officer. Life should have been great for Michele, but it wasn't.

Michele, totally enamored with police work, couldn't get enough of it or stop talking about it. Peter, Michele's husband, on the other hand, didn't like her choice of careers at all, and this disagreement led to a number of very heated discussions. Peter did not want her to be a police officer, period. However, being a police officer had always been Michele's dream. He wanted her to quit, and told her so. She was determined to stay, and told him so.

Finally, the disagreement about Michele's career choice became so heated, with neither side willing to back down, that Peter decided their marriage just wouldn't work any longer. However, obviously worried that he would lose custody of their son, Peter abducted Christopher and fled with him to Germany. Michele immediately started divorce proceedings.

On April 11, 1980, Peter returned to Florida, unbeknown to Michele. Catching her by surprise on the street, he suddenly brandished a .357 Magnum revolver. Michele, using her police training, attempted to get behind a parked car and pull her own revolver from an ankle holster. Peter, however, was on her before she could, and shot her five times, killing her. He then got into his car and drove away.

Responding police officers found Peter slumped in his car several blocks away. He had turned the gun on himself. Before he died, Peter taped a suicide message that said he had killed Michele because she loved her job more than him.

$$\gg$$

Readers may wonder if the problem in this anecdote is so rare as to be inconsequential. Unfortunately, the answer is no. This problem exists for many policewomen, although most times without such a tragic ending. For example, Liz Coffal told me in an interview that her husband, Robert Robinson, who was a sergeant on the Indianapolis Police Department when they met, almost didn't marry her for the same reason that had caused problems for Michele and Peter. "Robbie almost changed his mind about marrying me," Liz told me. "He said he thought I loved my job more than him."[2]

The reason policewomen (and policemen) love their jobs so much is because police work is both intoxicating and addictive. Car chases, tracking down suspects, breaking down doors, wrestling with people, and the many other activities that millions of television viewers and movie goers pay every day to experience vicariously usually only serve to fuel a police officer's need for more. Although these events can occasionally occur all in one shift or sometimes come weeks apart, police officers seldom get burned out on them. Police officers, instead, often become adrenalin junkies who wait anxiously for the next episode of excitement.

I recall the first time my wife, soon after being sworn in as a police officer, became involved in a high-speed car chase. At that time, she worked the 7 p.m. to 3 a.m. shift. Usually when she came home at the end of her shift (I was working day shift then), she tried to slip quietly into bed without waking me. However, that wasn't the case this night. Instead, she flipped on the overhead light and then sat down on the edge of the bed and told me every single detail of the chase, her breath raspy as she recalled the exhilarating excitement of the event. The very same thing happened on her first big arrest, her first fight, and so on. Although extremely difficult at 3 o'clock in the morning, I tried to act fascinated, knowing how important it was to her, even though I had been on the police department for over a dozen years by then and had already experienced these things many times myself.

Along with the excitement of police work, the job is also addictive because as a police officer you know you are really helping people. As a police officer, you know you are making a major difference in many people's lives. For example, in my career I saved several lives, rescued many other individuals from dangerous situations, and through my work changed the lives of many people for the better. It's a great feeling knowing that your job isn't meaningless, but is instead something extremely important. It's a great feeling knowing that you're making a difference in the world.

"This is the most fulfilling career anyone could have," said Captain Kerry Orpinuk of the Daytona Beach Police Department. She is her department's first female captain.[3]

"I absolutely love the career choice I made, instead of becoming an attorney," said another policewoman.[4]

"I love my job! I love police work!" said a female officer to a researcher conducting a study of successful policewomen.[5]

However, although most policewomen truly love their job to the point of it becoming an essential part of their identity, it is often very difficult for someone not involved in police work to understand all of this. And this is one of the reasons, I believe, that so many policewomen marry policemen. I doubt if I had been an office manager or maybe a teacher or an accountant I would have understood the adrenalin rush I knew my wife got from the incidents she woke me up at 3:00 a.m. to tell me about. And I doubt that I would have understood the extreme satisfaction and exhilaration my wife felt later when she became a sex crimes detective and put a child molester away for fifty years or so.

Police officers married to each other also understand some of the unique characteristics of the job. For example, they understand the nervousness an officer experiences before going to trial on a big case and the occasional set of the blues an officer gets from a particularly sad or gruesome case. And it is very important that they understand how crucial it is to let a police officer who works night shift sleep. A police officer's life can often depend on being alert and clear-headed, something getting only four or five hours of sleep won't do. My first wife, who wasn't a police officer, could never understand how I could still be in bed at noon, even though I hadn't gotten to bed until 7:30 or 8:00 a.m. Consequently, she would often become upset if I wouldn't get up to go to social events that took place in the late morning or early afternoon.

"Ever wonder why a lot of cops marry each other?" asked Sergeant Susan Grant of the Saskatoon, Canada, Police Department. "Cops come with a basic set of values . . . which gives you a common starting point as a couple."[6]

A research study conducted about the effects of stress on policewomen, and its influence on policewomen's families, found definite benefits to being married to a police officer. "[The results of this study] suggest that having a partner who has a shared understanding of some of the difficulties involved in police work can reduce the negative emotional outcomes associated with such work," said the authors of the study.[7]

For example, when my present wife worked as a child abuse detective, the police department psychologist met with her unit and counseled the detectives on the best way to deal with the stress of the many horrible and inhumane things they would see as child abuse detectives. He said they needed to talk to someone about it frequently. My wife, naturally, chose me. Every day, it seemed, she would come home and tell me about a more horrible case than the day before. Although this may have been good advice from the psychologist for the mental health of the child abuse detectives, I'm not sure the psychologist gave that much thought to the mental health of the people who had to hear about these cases. And I'm pretty certain that most non-police officers would not have been nearly as willing as I was to put up with the almost daily onrush of horror stories. However, having been there, I understood my wife's need to unload, and so I tried to be as supportive as possible.

Experience has also shown that marriages between police officers work so well so often because they don't raise any ego or masculine identity problems for the husband of a policewoman. On the other hand, many non-policemen, who might think it will be exciting to have a relationship with a policewoman, can nevertheless later be bothered by the fact that it is the woman, not them, who packs the gun, carries the badge, and has the authority to arrest or even take a life if necessary.

I couldn't find any statistics, other than one study of 815 policewomen, concerning how many policewomen are married to policemen. In the one study I did find, the number was a little over 50 percent.[8] This is about the same number of policewomen, or perhaps a little lower, as the numbers who are married to policemen at the Indianapolis Police Department. Also, when researching this book, in the many anecdotes I came across involving policewomen I discovered that the majority of them are married to policemen. Chief Montejo said,

My husband is a police officer, and that really does help. For me, it works, and because of being married to a police officer I got a lot of support. My mother, however, wasn't quite as enthusiastic at first. We were in the car when I told her about wanting to be a police officer, and she almost drove off the road. But then later, when she found out that it was really what I wanted to do, she became very supportive.[9]

Another policewoman who is married to a policeman sums it up:

> One morning at around 3 a.m. the phone rang. It was the police station, and they wanted my husband. He is . . . on the bomb squad and he also investigates high-end sexual assaults [sexual assaults involving some other crime, such as robbery or a vicious physical attack]. . . . I lifted my head slightly off the pillow and said, "Is it sex or bombs?" He calmly replied, "Sex." I yawned and with a sleepy goodbye, he was off to his call.[10]

Although I have given a lot of positives in this chapter for the idea of policewomen marrying policemen, I don't want to imply that policewomen cannot have successful marriages except to policemen because I know of a number of marriages of policewomen to non-police officers that do appear to work very well. However, I also know of a number of marriages that didn't work well because the husband simply couldn't understand his wife's love of police work, and the strange hours and eccentricities that come with the job, to say nothing of the strong bond that exists between police officers. Also, many of these marriages haven't worked because the husband's ego and masculine identity weren't secure enough. It takes a very secure man to stay in a relationship knowing that if something criminal goes down he will have to stand aside and let his wife take care of it. And, as I said previously, it takes a very secure man not to be bothered by the fact that it is his wife, not him, who carries the badge, who packs the gun, and who has the authority to arrest or even to take a life if necessary.

Of course, this also works in reverse. Often the marriages of policemen to women other than policewomen end in divorce because the wives don't understand the strange hours, they can't relate to the exhilaration their husbands get from the job, and many times they don't understand the very close bond that police officers develop with each other. When individuals have to daily depend on each other to back each other up, and to perhaps even save each others' lives, an extraordinarily close bond forms between these individuals.

And because policewomen are now a regular part of police patrol, this close bond involves them. This, as might be expected, can cause problems in policemen's marriages. In Wilmington, North Carolina, according to an article in the *Wilmington Star-News*, when policewomen first went on street patrol, "Officers' wives were sent to a psychiatrist from Raleigh to learn how to deal with a woman working with their husbands all day."[11] According to an article in *Ladies Home Journal*, "In some cities, the wives of policemen have protested that the assignment of women to patrol partnerships would endanger their husbands or tempt them into sexual liaisons with their female colleagues."[12]

Police administrators also know how close this bond can become. As we talked about in chapter 5, when policewomen first went out on street patrol in Philadelphia, police department administrators forbade them from ever riding in a police car with a policeman because of the fear of intimate relationships forming.

Again, as I said previously, I don't want readers to think that I'm saying there aren't any happy, working marriages between policewomen and non-policemen because I know of a number of cases in which it is true. However, to make the marriage successful takes a man with a very secure ego and a strong masculine identity.

Unfortunately, however, there are an awful lot of men in our country who aren't that secure in their ego or masculine identity; it is just as unfortunate that this concern about their masculinity is why a number of these men become police officers. They hope that the badge and its authority will bolster their frail ego and masculinity. But many times it doesn't, and their insecurity then often leads them to become involved in excessive force incidents on duty and in domestic violence situations off duty.

Most readers will likely be surprised to know that, even though police officers deal with domestic violence on a daily basis (it is the most common run police officers receive), this problem is present in many of their own relationships. Nationwide, 10 to 20 percent of all marriages reportedly experience domestic violence, and several studies have found that domestic violence is present in at least this many and perhaps more police marriages.

There are many explanations given for this, but the one that makes the most sense to me is that police officers, in their jobs, are used to giving orders and having them obeyed. And if they are not obeyed, police officers will then use force and increase the force level until they are obeyed. Regrettably, this increase in force often comes much quicker, and usually with much less justification, for those officers with weak egos and masculine identities, often leading to excessive force complaints from citizens. And sadly, this behavior many times carries over into police officers' personal relationships, and is the perfect recipe for domestic violence.

Unfortunately, for many years, police departments kept this problem of domestic violence a family secret within the department. Whenever the department received a domestic violence run to the home of a police officer, a supervisor would usually respond and take the officer aside and tell him to knock it off, while another officer would try to comfort the wife, but at the same time make her aware of the dire consequences to her husband's career and economic potential if their situation wasn't kept under wraps. Consequently, reports were seldom ever filed, and, except in the most extreme cases, no arrests were ever made. To show the depth of this problem, in a twenty-two-month period the Los Angeles Police Department reportedly received 508 reports of domestic violence involving their own police officers.[13] "Since the earliest days of law enforcement, domestic violence in police families was considered an officer's personal business, one of those private realms into which departmental administrators chose not to involve themselves," said retired Chicago Homicide Lieutenant Dennis Banahan, who responded to many such calls during his career.[14]

Readers may wonder how this part of the discussion fits the subject matter of policewomen. Actually, it affects policewomen in several ways. For one, policewomen can often be sent on runs to the homes of police officers who are involved in domestic violence. Once there, the policewomen are faced with a dilemma. Should they support and protect the abuser, a person they might have to depend on to protect them on the street in the future, or should they do what they would do if the perpetrator of the domestic violence wasn't a police officer? An article in *Police* magazine very succinctly states this problem:

> Officers who respond to police-involved domestic violence calls face an emotional tug-of-war between protecting the abuser, a fellow cop, and sympathizing with the victim. Since the overwhelming majority of officers who abuse their loved ones are male and their victims female, it's especially hard on female cops who respond to these calls.[15]

What then can a policewoman do in these cases? If she arrests the abusing officer, she runs the risk of breaking her bond with the other officers on the department. The relationship can be irretrievably damaged. As I've talked about earlier, police officers form a very close-knit community, and arresting a member of the community can possibly lead to ostracism. But on the other hand, a policewoman can feel worthless if she doesn't do something.

The answer to this problem lies with police department administrators. They must make it an unbreakable departmental rule that a supervisor will respond to all calls of police-involved domestic violence, and that the case will be handled no differently than any other domestic violence case. In this way the onus is taken off of everyone.

But of course we shouldn't suppose that it is only male police officers who are the aggressors in domestic violence situations. Policewomen are too. For example, in March 2008, the Miami Police Department arrested one of its own policewomen, a seventeen-year veteran, Yatha LeGrand, for domestic violence. However, the results of this case aside, like male police officers involved in such incidents, domestic violence runs involving policewomen as the aggressors also often don't end in an arrest or even a report being made about them. And consequently, the problem is never solved.

An even more ominous problem can be when the policewomen themselves are the victims of domestic violence, often as a result of their job and its effect on their significant others. Readers may doubt the frequency of this, but unfortunately many such incidents occur. For example, the husband of New York City police officer Milta Bruetsch followed her to her brother's house in Piermont, New York. He dragged her out of the house and shot her five times, killing her. Milta had reportedly fled to her brother's house to escape her husband, who had been physically abusing her. In a similar case, the estranged husband of Louisville policewoman Gwendolyn Downs shot and killed her, and then killed himself. Officer Downs had allegedly earlier reported abuse by her husband.

Many readers may find it hard to believe that a policewoman could be the victim of domestic violence. After all, she has the same physical and self-defense training as a male officer. Why would she allow herself to become a victim? Why wouldn't she report it or try to stop it?

There are a number of reasons for not reporting it. The first and most likely reason is shame. How can a policewoman admit that she is the victim of domestic violence? After all, she responds yearly to hundreds of cases of domestic violence and stops them. Why can't she stop her own? Also, as a police officer, she is always in control. She decides what is going to happen in every situation she is called to. How then can she admit that she can't control her own private life? With all the problems she is called to solve in her job as a police officer, how can she admit that she has an insolvable problem in her own life?

In addition, a female officer may also be afraid that if she reports being the victim of domestic violence, others will question her ability to protect citizens if she can't protect herself. Policewomen know only too well how vulnerable they will become if they report domestic violence. People will almost certainly question their judgment for getting themselves involved in such a situation, and many policewomen fear it will affect the future of their careers.

And of course if a policewoman grew up in a home where domestic violence occurred, she may be conditioned to simply tolerate it. She may believe that all marriages are like this, and she must simply put up with it like her mother did.

But most important, a policewoman also knows that if she calls 911 to report domestic violence, the responding officers will then know all of the intimacies of her problem. Although an official report may not be generated, the responding officers will still know. And although one would hope that these details would stay private, police departments are huge rumor mills, and this type of information does, and likely will, get out.

Finally, as for stopping the abuse, a policewoman may realize that the domestic violence in her relationship is occurring because her partner's ego is suffering due to the power and authority of her job. Therefore, she also realizes that any attempt by her to fight back will likely only bruise her partner's ego even more and lead to escalated, and possibly even deadly, violence.

Although, as we talked about previously, domestic violence involving policewomen can have many causes, one of the causes that has been the subject of several research projects is the stress that policewomen regularly undergo because of their job, and the effect this stress has on their personal relationships. One of the studies, undertaken by Professor Don Kurtz of Kansas State University, found that although family can help a male police officer deal with the stress of his job, families often have the opposite effect on female officers. Although most families accept that a male police officer, because of his work, may have to miss important family events, families are not always as tolerant and forgiving for female police officers. Policewomen must often deal with stress at work, and then come home to even more stress as a wife and mother. "Women settle into the role of caretaker and come home to a second shift," said Professor Kurtz.[16]

"I still get crap when I have to take time off to take care of my kids," said Officer Lori Connelly of the Phoenix Police Department. "And as a woman it's expected I do it to take care of them or I'm a bad mom, but then they say that I can't be counted on because I drop everything to take care of my kids."[17]

Another study of stress, this one by Professor John Violante of the University of Buffalo, found that one-fourth of all the policewomen studied had thoughts of suicide, which is about twice as high as the general public, and three times as high as other city workers. This level of distress cannot help but affect any personal relationships these police-women are involved in. "Psychological survival is sometimes more difficult in policing than survival in the street," said Professor Violante.[18]

Although this information about suicidal thoughts may be surprising to some readers, it isn't to most police officers. Police work, although exhilarating and intoxicating, can also have a negative side to it in that police officers often see horrible things that average people cannot even imagine. These events can many times prey on an officer's mind, which, of course, adds stress to the police officer's life. Also, because police work, even with its bad side, is still so exhilarating and intoxicating, it can many times interfere with, or even fatally damage, personal relationships, because it can seem to loved ones that the job is more important than the relationship. As a result, police officers are often pressured by loved ones to give up a job they truly love, which then just adds even more stress.

Consequently, because of all the stress that police officers can be under, the suicide rate among police officers is very high. One study, for example, found the suicide rate among police officers, male and female, to be three times as high as for the general public.[19] Importantly, however, this problem exists not only because of the intense stress many police officers are under, but also because most police officers fear that asking for the help that might eliminate, or at least lower, their stress will be seen as a sign of weakness and will affect their careers. And, unfortunately, with the increase of policewomen on police departments, and their movement into all areas of police work, this problem of unresolved stress and a reluctance to ask for help has simply spread to them.

"Many officers feel that referral to a mental health professional would mean the loss of their jobs," said the authors of an article about police suicide. "Officers fear that if help is sought, employment and economic security will be threatened."[20]

This is not a hopeless problem, however. A method that has been shown to be effective in a number of police departments for dealing with this situation is that, at the first sign of any problems that might indicate suicidal thoughts or intentions, police department supervisors, who are trained to be alert for these signs, order the police officer to see a mental health professional. This then solves the problem of a reluctance to seek help, as the officer has no choice.

As another suicide prevention program, many police departments today make it routine that officers must, without exception, see a mental health professional if they become involved in any highly stressful situation that can lead to emotional problems, such as a police-action shooting (a police officer shoots someone), an auto accident in which someone is killed or seriously injured, or whenever officers become involved in an extremely gruesome case. In addition to this, many police departments today also allow police officers to seek counseling from a department-approved mental health professional without having to report it, and without the police department receiving any notice of the identity of the officers seeking help. When I was commander of the Indianapolis Police Department's Personnel Branch, I would monthly approve payment for mental health services without ever knowing who was receiving them.

As might be imagined, the stresses of police work that we've talked about so far can have a very detrimental effect on any policewoman's personal life. If she can't find coping mechanisms to lessen their impact, they can damage her personal relationships. And although many people may wonder why a policewoman doesn't just heed her loved ones' entreaties to quit the job, it's not that easy. Despite the stress and horrible things police officers see, the excitement of the job, its worthiness, and the camaraderie with fellow officers far, far outweigh any negatives of the job.

Earlier in this chapter we talked quite a bit about the personal relationship problems of married policewomen. Unmarried policewomen also face unique problems, many of which don't affect most other single women. A policewoman's job, for instance, can be a real deficit when venturing into the dating scene. Earlier I discussed the ego problems that can develop when a policewoman marries a non-police officer; it can also be very threatening to a man's ego to date a policewoman. Although it might sound exciting at first to date a policewoman, any man venturing into this must be prepared for a relationship different from most.

"There is still an odd fascination with women in law enforcement," said Sergeant Betsy Brantner Smith, who, before she retired, worked at the Naperville, Illinois, Police Department. "While you're dating you've got to kind of wade through that. It can be very intimidating for the person who is dating a female cop who carries a gun and has the constitutional authority to take a life."[21]

And of course, if a female police officer becomes seriously involved with someone who is not a police officer that person may have difficulty relating to the job she does and her feelings about it. "You're an accountant and you're telling her about your day," said Smith, "and she's talking about the guy she tasered and the active shooting training she went to or she's talking about her new AR-15 and the training she's going to. Normal people don't understand us and they look at us and think 'this girl is a little off.'"[22]

Sergeant Susan Grant said,

Finding a date when you are a policewoman can sometimes prove to be difficult. Unlike policemen, we don't have "badge bunnies" chasing us. You see, women love men in uniform; it is masculine and authoritative, courageous and strong. Women in the same uniform carry similar qualities, which usually aren't considered attractive qualities for a female— unless you are wearing a nurse's uniform rather than a police one.[23]

("Badge bunnies" are police groupies. Badge bunnies are women look-ing for sexual encounters with policemen. All large police departments have dozens and sometimes hundreds of them.)

Unfortunately, as I've mentioned, police officers, as a part of their job, often witness horrible, tragic events that ordinary people don't. As a consequence, in order to deal emotionally with these events, to keep them from preying on an officer's mind, police officers must have some sort of coping mechanism. The way most police officers deal with them is through "graveyard humor." Police officers make jokes and laugh about things that average people would be disgusted or aghast at. This joking and laughing helps police officers deal emotionally with these events by distancing themselves from them through humor. Yet, as might be imagined, a policewoman's date can be appalled at the things she thinks are funny, and will likely believe she is a ghoul for laughing about others' tragedies.

However, even more damaging to potential personal relationships is the fact that good cops are always suspicious of everyone, and distrust-ful of anything people tell them. This simply comes with the job. But, as might be imagined, this doesn't work well with new relationships. In addition, police officers are used to giving orders and having them obeyed, again hardly a trait that will help further new personal relation-ships. "One of the great paradoxes of police work is that those same habits that often make for being a good cop make for being a poor mate or parent," said Dr. Ellen Kirschman, a consulting psychologist to police departments.[24]

As we have talked about several times in this book, the problems that policewomen face are not confined to just the United States. "I joined the police against my father's wishes," said G. Manimozhi of the Tiruvarur district of India. "Growing up in our village, I was always told what women can and cannot do. This has given me a new level of self-confidence. I know now a woman can handle any situation."[25] A woman interviewed about policewomen in the Czech Republic said, "If I have a daughter one day and she ever considers becoming a policewoman I will do my best to talk her out of such nonsense."[26]

Of course, as these two examples show, it's not just husbands and boyfriends who can cause emotional relationship problems for police-women. Often, the families of policewomen—parents, children, siblings, and so on—also don't understand the fascination with the job, and can oppose a policewoman's choice of careers, causing considerable emotional stress.

"My son hates the idea of me becoming a policewoman," said a woman in an Internet parenting forum. "My son (6 years old,) is scared for me . . . tears come out of his eyes. I have to prepare him because next year I am starting my training, and I don't want to let go because being a policewoman is my dream."[27]

Liz Coffal told me in an interview, "I had an uncle who steadfastly believed that women should not be police officers. He never approved of my job, and once I went out on the street he wouldn't talk about it."[28] Interestingly, Betty Blankenship, Liz's partner, wasn't overly excited when she found out that her daughter wanted to join the Indianapolis Police Department. "I really had mixed emotions about it," Betty said. She told a reporter that she worried because she believed it was more dangerous now on the street than it was when she went out.[29]

Even my own father, who had three sons and a daughter-in-law on the Indianapolis Police Department, didn't approve of or support my wife's career choice. Because of the danger and the type of people and incidents police officers deal with, he didn't believe women should be police officers.

Many family members, I've found, like Betty and my father, oppose women becoming police officers because they believe the work is much too dangerous for women. And although there is no denying that the job is more dangerous than most of the average jobs women have, with police officers being three times as likely to be killed as average citizens, it is still by no means the most dangerous job a woman can have. The top ten most dangerous jobs in 2008, all of which employ women, were (in rank order from first to tenth) logger; pilot; fisher; iron or steel worker; garbage collector; farmer or rancher; roofer; electrical power installer or repairer; sales, delivery, or other truck driver; and taxi driver or chauffer.[30]

That policing is not as dangerous as some other jobs, however, can be of little comfort to the family members of potential or active policewomen who still believe that police work, because of the danger, is simply not a job for women. Although this opposition from family members often diminishes after enough time passes and the family members see that the policewoman in their family can take care of herself, it is still often just more stress that a policewoman must bear.

As shown previously, police work is not the most dangerous job women can have. Yet I can't assure family members that policewomen don't face any danger at all in their jobs. The truth is that the job can be very dangerous at times. This danger, however, is one of the reasons many people are drawn to police work, and it is one of the reasons they stay in the job against all opposition. And unfortunately, as we will see in the next chapter, many policewomen have paid the ultimate price for accepting the danger of police work.

## ⑨

# THE SUPREME SACRIFICE

On September 20, 1974, in Washington, D.C., only about six blocks from the White House, a fleeing bank robber shot and killed a police officer. Unfortunately this sort of incident happens often enough in our country that its newsworthiness is usually only good for a day or two, but this event was different. This murder, rather than just a passing news story, became a landmark in law enforcement history. The first police-woman on street patrol had been killed in the line of duty.

This murder, occurring just a little over six years after Liz and Betty first rolled out in Car 47, hadn't been totally unexpected. Because by 1974 so many cities in the United States had policewomen in patrol cars, police administrators all across the country had known this event was coming, that it would happen eventually. But still, most hoped it wouldn't happen in their community.

The murdered policewoman, Gail A. Cobb, had come from a law enforcement family. Her father had served in the Washington, D.C., Department of Corrections since 1955, and in 1974 held the rank of captain. Gail had decided to join the Washington, D.C., Police Department in October 1973. Washington, D.C., at that time had been following the growing trend in the United States of assigning policewomen to street patrol, and consequently had for several years been actively recruiting women, even lowering their height requirement to bring in more applicants. Upon Officer Gail Cobb's graduation from the training academy in April 1974, the police department assigned the twenty-four-year-old to a walking beat.

Five months later, on the morning of September 20, 1974, two Washington, D.C., police officers spotted a couple of men acting suspiciously as they walked toward a savings and loan company. The men wore construction overalls and carried a bricklayer's bag, which the police would later discover contained a sawed-off shotgun. The police had earlier been tipped off that two men would rob the savings and loan that day.

When the officers approached the two men and asked for identification, one of the men jerked the sawed-off shotgun out of the bricklayer's bag and pointed it at them. The closest officer grabbed the shotgun and shoved it away. The two men then fled on foot, firing several shots at the pursuing officers.

Officer Gail Cobb, on patrol nearby, received information that one of the fleeing men had run into a parking garage at 1925 L Street, N.W. Officer Cobb was at that moment at 20th and L Street. She ran down the sidewalk and into the garage, confronting a man later identified as John William Bryant, who was attempting to take off the green worker's coveralls he was wearing. Officer Cobb ordered Bryant to put his hands on the wall. She then got on her walkie-talkie and asked for assistance. Bryant, however, instead of complying, spun around and fired a gun at Officer Cobb. The bullet went through her wrist and walkie-talkie and into her heart, killing her.

Officers responded quickly and arrested Bryant at the scene. The other man the police had pursued, John C. Dortch, surrendered through an attorney the next day. Dortch, a college graduate and a former Army officer who had served in Vietnam, had been the mastermind behind a plan to rob a number of financial institutions in order to support a group he called the "Black Mafia." Dortch envisioned this group as using the money they would get from the robberies to bankroll black businesses. Unfortunately, the officer killed in this event, Gail A. Cobb, was also black.

Dortch and Bryant both pled guilty to their part in Officer Cobb's death. A court sentenced each man to a term of fifteen years to life in prison. Five other members of the "Black Mafia" also received prison sentences for their part in the conspiracy.

On September 24, 1974, more than four thousand people attended Officer Cobb's funeral at the Holy Comforter Catholic Church in northeast Washington, D.C. Police officers from all over the nation attended, and a funeral procession of over five hundred police cars escorted Officer Cobb's body to the Lincoln Memorial Cemetery.

"Something else happened last Friday that changed the course of history," said police chaplain R. Joseph Dooley at Officer Cobb's funeral. "As the first policewoman in the nation to give her life in the line of duty, her death established the fact that criminals make no distinction between the sexes."[1]

≫

As mentioned previously, Officer Gail Cobb's death marked a milestone in law enforcement history. The first policewoman on street patrol had been killed in the line of duty. And, as also mentioned, everyone in law enforcement had known that this event would eventually happen, and all had waited with dread for it to come. Actually, however, looking at the yearly statistics for police officers killed in the line of duty, it is probably more surprising that it took more than six years for this event to occur.

The FBI first began keeping statistics on the number of police officers killed in the line of duty in 1960, and by the early 1970s the number averaged more than 175 a year, with the mid-1970s being a particularly deadly time for police officers. In the year before Officer Cobb's death, 266 police officers had died in the line of duty. In the year of her death, 280 officers died. Consequently, by 1974, everyone knew that a policewoman line-of-duty death was already long overdue.

≫

Although Officer Cobb became the first policewoman in the United States to be killed in the line of duty and this event generated considerable publicity, she wasn't the first woman employed by a police department to be murdered on the job. That distinction belongs to Anna Hart, a matron for the Hamilton County, Ohio, Sheriff's Department.

On July 24, 1916, forty-five-year-old Anna Hart had just finished her shift as a matron at the county jail in Cincinnati and was walking though the jail getting ready to go home. She thought that the cellblock she was in would be deserted because it was dinnertime and all of the inmates should have been in the dining hall. However, one inmate, twenty-six-year-old Reuben Ellis, had slipped out of line while being marched to dinner. He hid behind a curtain and then waylaid Anna Hart with a metal rod when she walked by, fracturing her skull. He had earlier confided to other inmates that he intended to attack a matron, grab her key ring, and then make his escape. However, employees at the jail found Anna's body before Reuben could carry out his plan and get away. Investigators later found Anna's keys in a bucket where Reuben had thrown them. They also found the weapon, which had been a piece of Reuben's bed.

To everyone's surprise, including the defense attorney's, Reuben's first trial ended in a hung jury (a jury that cannot agree on a verdict). The jury in his second trial (which took place only six weeks after the conclusion of his first trial) spent only forty minutes finding him guilty of murder. The jury also made no recommendation for mercy. Consequently, on February 6, 1917, less seven months after Anna Hart's murder, Reuben died in the electric chair.

☰

Anna Hart was just one of five matrons killed by inmates attempting to escape before John William Bryant shot and killed Officer Gail Cobb in 1974. And yet, even though the shooting death of Officer Cobb generated considerable publicity, she was not the first female police employee to be shot to death on the job. That event occurred three years earlier in 1971 when a visitor to the jail in Detroit, Maggie Pugh, smuggled in a .22-caliber firearm. Pugh, a woman with a criminal record who was on parole at the time, wanted to free Elaine Stanley, an inmate at the jail. Pugh shot and killed fifty-six-year-old jail matron Marta Shanaman when she refused to open the door to the area holding Stanley.

"On that Sunday, December 12th, I was working two floors below 'Shanty,' answering 911 emergency calls in Communications," said a coworker of Marta Shanaman, "when I heard the 'emergency' buzzer go off; then a radio alert 'Officer down on 8th floor Detention,' and suddenly I had a sense of dread—I knew Shanty was on duty."[2]

Quickly responding officers captured Pugh and Stanley before they had a chance to escape. A court later sentenced Pugh to life imprisonment for the murder of Marta Shanaman.

Marta Shanaman holds the distinction of being the first female civilian police employee to be shot to death on the job (the three matrons murdered between Anna Hart and Marta Shanaman had been beaten to death) and Gail Cobb was the first policewoman to be shot to death. However, they would be just the first of many. As of July 2009, along with Marta Shanaman and Officer Gail Cobb, seventy-nine other female police employees have been shot to death in the line of duty.

≫

Unfortunately, although it took six years for a policewoman on patrol to be killed on the job, Officer Gail Cobb turned out to be only the first of many policewomen killed in the line of duty. As policewomen began taking on more and more dangerous jobs in police departments, such as street patrol and detective positions, the deaths of these policewomen began to mount. By July 2009, the National Law Enforcement Memorial in Washington, D.C., reported that it had 235 women listed on its rolls as dying in the line of duty.

Officer Cobb died in a shootout with a criminal, which is the manner most people likely visualize when they think of a police officer being killed in the line of duty. However, another part of police work can also be extremely dangerous and kills many police officers every year: driving a police vehicle at high speeds.

≫

At just a little after midnight on July 27, 1977, thirty-year-old Fairfax County, Virginia, police officer Karen Jean Bassford received a Code 1 run on a burglary in progress. This meant she needed to get to the scene as quickly as possible. She jumped into her police car and sped off toward the address. With her police car's emergency equipment operating, Officer Bassford lost control of her vehicle going around a curve, slid more than 450 feet, and then crashed into a utility pole. The crash threw Officer Bassford from the car and she died at the scene. Officer Bassford had served on the Fairfax County Police Department for a little over a year, and had earlier served as a police officer in Arlington County, Virginia, for a little over two years.

Unfortunately, as often happens in law enforcement, the run the dispatcher had sent Officer Bassford on turned out to be a false alarm. An elderly resident had heard a noise and called the police. Investigators later found no signs of a burglary.

Along with the hazard of sharp curves, other unexpected dangers can also occur when operating a police vehicle at high speeds. On June 20, 1984, twenty-two-year-old police officer Doreen A. Tomlinson of the Pawtucket, Rhode Island, Police Department had been looking for a car reported to be driving erratically in a residential neighborhood. It had been described as a white Cadillac. Suddenly, a white Cadillac zoomed by her at high speed. Officer Tomlinson turned on her police car's emergency equipment and sped off in pursuit.

Unfortunately, the erratic driver fled onto a road under construction and Officer Tomlinson's car hit a patch of unpaved road and she lost control. Her police car struck a parked back hoe and then a utility pole. Although rushed to the hospital, Officer Tomlinson died six days later without regaining consciousness. No one knows what happened to the white Cadillac she had been pursuing.

The Rhode Island General Assembly, following Officer Tomlinson's death, passed a measure honoring her. They renamed the athletic fields on Daggett Avenue in Pawtucket the Doreen A. Tomlinson Memorial Fields.

Sometimes the danger of high-speed police driving is not the road, but other drivers. An Indianapolis policewoman lost her life discovering this. At around 3:00 a.m. on August 17, 1993, twenty-eight-year-old Officer Teresa Hawkins received a run from the dispatcher that an ambulance crew was having trouble with a patient and needed help right away. While in route to her run at high speed, a drunk driver ran a stop sign and struck Officer Hawkins's police car broadside, sending it over the curb and smashing it through a utility pole. The crash had such force that Officer Hawkins's car, after going through the utility pole, then crashed into a house. Officer Hawkins died several hours later at the hospital.

The driver of the vehicle that struck Officer Hawkins's police car, Elvis Lacy, fled the accident scene on foot, but police officers quickly apprehended him. His blood alcohol level was 0.191, nearly twice the level needed at that time to sustain the charge of drunk driving. Lacy later pled guilty to Officer Hawkins's death and a judge sentenced him to eight years in prison.

⁂

Although there are obviously many dangers inherent in police work, readers wouldn't expect that a police officer's partner would be one of these. Sadly, that isn't always the case. Being armed and involved in highly stressful situations can often lead to deadly accidents. Thirty-nine-year-old Constance Worland of the Los Angeles County Sheriff's Department became a victim of one of these accidents.

On May 2, 1981, Officer Worland and her partner received a "man with a gun" run in a high crime neighborhood known as Scottsdale Estates. They jumped into their police car and sped off toward the address. Once there, however, a witness gave them a new location where the suspect might be hiding. At this first stop, Officer Worland's partner had reportedly taken the police car's shotgun from its floorboard rack, put a shell in the chamber, and then clicked off the safety. Unfortunately, he apparently put the gun back into the floorboard rack with the safety still off and a shell still in the chamber, an extremely dangerous condition.

According to a report of the case, "When Connie and her partner reached the new location and she was exiting the vehicle, her partner grabbed the shotgun, still loaded from the initial contact, and it accidentally discharged, striking her in the low back area."[3] The shotgun's stock apparently struck the steering column as Officer Worland's partner removed it, and the gun went off, striking Officer Worland. She died several hours afterward. Tests conducted later on the shotgun showed that a blow to the stock of the gun, such as it striking the steering column, would consistently make it fire. As a result, the prosecutor filed no charges in the case.

Although this may seem like an event that is unlikely to happen very often, unfortunately it isn't. A number of police officers have been shot and killed by other police officers during the stress of a chase, a physical struggle, or a shootout. Panic and stress can set in during these types of incidents, and anything can happen. And, as I show in the following section, even agencies such as the FBI aren't immune from such events.

The FBI, on October 4, 1985, received a tip that Kenneth Barrett, a man wanted for an armored car robbery and the shooting of a police officer, was staying in an apartment in Phoenix, Arizona. Consequently, the local FBI office made plans to arrest him. Thirty-three-year-old FBI Special Agent Robin Ahrens went along as one of twelve agents who set up around the apartment. The plan the agents had drawn up was to wait until Barrett came outside and then to make the arrest. However, one of the agents on the detail, going up to the apartment alone to check on something, unexpectedly confronted Barrett as the suspect left the apartment. The agent made the decision to go ahead and arrest Barrett before he could flee back into the apartment, where there were likely weapons. A struggle ensued and the agent's gun went off, sending the rest of the agents scrambling toward the arrest scene.

Two of the FBI agents who arrived to assist the fellow agent saw the shadowy figure of a woman holding a gun running toward them. Later saying that they thought it might be Barrett's girlfriend, the two agents shouted for her to stop, and, when she didn't, they opened fire. Unfortunately, the approaching figure turned out to be Special Agent Ahrens, rushing to assist in the arrest. The agents fired eleven shots at her, striking her three times and killing her.

According to an article in the *New York Times*, "The Maricopa County Attorney's Office, after a meeting of its shooting review board, issued a statement saying the agents committed 'no act which warrants prosecution.'"[4]

The FBI, however, didn't agree and fired one of the agents. The other agent resigned rather than be fired. An investigation of the event showed that the agents knew that Barrett's girlfriend was pregnant, while Agent Ahrens was slim and fit. In honor of Special Agent Ahrens, the FBI building in Phoenix has been renamed the Robin L. Ahrens Building.

≫

When most readers recall the events of September 11, 2001, along with remembering the many civilian deaths, they likely also think with sorrow of all the firefighters and police officers who lost their lives trying to save individuals trapped in the World Trade Center. Although few people are probably aware of it, a female police officer also gave her life that day.

Police officer Moira Smith had joined the New York City Police Department in 1988, transferring to the 13th Precinct in March 1996. Like many public safety workers in New York City on September 11, 2001, she rushed to the scene of the terrorist attack, ready to do her part to save innocent lives. Reportedly, she was one of the first police officers to arrive at the scene of the World Trade Center tragedy. Moira immediately joined in the rescue, leading bleeding and bewildered people out of the smoke-filled towers.

This was not the first time Officer Smith had risked her life to save others. On August 27, 1991, the New York City Police Department had awarded her the Distinguished Duty Medal for repeatedly risking her life saving injured passengers following a subway crash. "She was the first uniformed officer on the scene," said her husband, New York City police officer Jim Smith. "We spent 12 hours pulling people out."[5]

A photograph taken on September 11 of Officer Moira Smith leading a businessman out of the World Trade Center, his face covered with blood, flashed across news media outlets that day in 2001. What few people who saw this picture know is that immediately after the photographer took this photo, Officer Smith rushed back into the damaged South Tower to bring down a lady from the third floor who was having an asthma attack. Before she could, however, the tower collapsed and killed her. It would be six months before rescue workers would recover Officer Smith's body.

The New York City Police Department posthumously presented Officer Moira Smith with its highest award, the Medal of Honor. Ironically, when she and her husband Jim had had their first child two years earlier, she had transferred from a street narcotics squad to a much safer community-policing unit.

"[O]n a number of occasions she had come out of the World Trade Center, carrying people out, then gone back in," said Lieutenant Charles Barbuti of the 13th Precinct. "She had the opportunity to leave and she chose not to."[6]

⪢

As we have talked about, police work, by its nature, can be an extremely hazardous occupation at times. Police officers often come in contact with dangerous criminals, highly stressed and battling intimates, intoxicated and drugged individuals, and many other people prone to violence. But many times, the most dangerous people police officers deal with are the mentally ill. This is not to infer that most mentally ill people are dangerous, but the ones citizens call the police over usually are. These individuals are extremely dangerous for the police to deal with because it is extraordinarily difficult to predict what they'll do. One moment calm, the next they can fly into a deadly rage.

⪢

Twenty-four-year-old New Orleans police officer Nicola Diane Cotton, at around 9:30 a.m. on February 2, 2008, pulled her police car into a small strip mall in Central City, a crime-ridden and impoverished area of New Orleans. She had received a radio run about a suspicious man there possibly wanted for rape. In the mall, she found forty-four-year-old Bernel P. Johnson sitting on the curb. What Officer Cotton didn't know was that Johnson had a long history of violence and mental illness.

A store surveillance camera showed Officer Cotton approaching Johnson and speaking with him. Then suddenly, a struggle broke out. Officer Cotton fought valiantly, even though she was only half the size of Johnson. The struggle between them lasted for seven minutes. The video showed Johnson choking Officer Cotton, hitting her with her baton, and then finally grabbing her .40-caliber Glock pistol from its holster.

Although Officer Cotton managed to radio for help, Johnson emptied the Glock pistol, all fifteen shots, into her, killing her. When help finally arrived, the officers said Johnson calmly handed over Officer Cotton's pistol and surrendered peacefully.

Reportedly, just a few weeks earlier, on January 4, 2008, Johnson had been declared mentally ill and dangerous, and committed to a mental health facility. For an unexplained reason, even though he had made threats to kill a police officer, the facility released him several weeks later.

Mental health officials wouldn't comment on the reason for Johnson's release, but one possible explanation given was that several years earlier Hurricane Katrina had drastically reduced the number of mental health facilities in New Orleans. Consequently, bed space for the mentally disturbed had become almost nonexistent. By February 2008, the situation hadn't improved much. In addition to the lack of bed space, however, this dearth of mental health facilities in New Orleans also meant that many mentally disturbed individuals in the area, such as Johnson, could no longer get their medication. Still, this explanation didn't sit well with those who knew Officer Cotton.

"The State of Louisiana had ample time to figure out this guy," said psychologist James Arey, commander of the New Orleans Police Department Crisis Negotiation Team. "And because they weren't doing their job, this officer, my friend, died."[7]

New Orleans Police Superintendent Warren Riley spoke at Officer Cotton's funeral. "She truly is a hero. She was doing a job that few can do and few would consider doing."[8]

Although all of the incidents we have talked about in this chapter have been tragic events, some readers might argue that many of them only happened because it was a woman rather than a man involved. This is not true. Every event discussed in this chapter has happened to male officers dozens or even hundreds of times. As Jill Hayes, a psychologist who counsels police officers, said, "Sometimes you can do everything right and the worst thing still happens."[9]

Officer Cobb's murder, discussed at the beginning of this chapter, was a milestone in law enforcement history. On August 9, 2004, law enforcement, unfortunately, reached another milestone. On that day, the two-hundredth female police employee died in the line of duty. On that day, a mentally disturbed man shot and killed twenty-seven-year-old LaToya Johnson in New Orleans. Officer Johnson and her partner had been attempting to serve commitment papers on thirty-eight-year-old Chester Solomon. Mr. Solomon's family had requested his commitment because they said he was mentally unstable and wouldn't take his medication. The police discovered later that he had possibly murdered a family member just before killing Officer Johnson.

As bad as the events are that we've talked about in this chapter, things aren't improving that much for policewomen. The year 2008 turned out to be one of the deadliest years on record for policewomen in the United States, with fifteen female officers killed in the line of duty. The only other year to tie that number was 2002. Interestingly, the overall number of police officers killed in the United States in 2008, 140, was the second lowest number in forty years. However, what this statistic also means is that for the first time more than 10 percent of all the police officers killed in the line of duty were women.

As we've discussed in other chapters, policewomen in foreign countries seldom fare any better than those in the United States. Consequently, policewomen in foreign countries are at just as much risk as those in the United States. In November 2005, for example, an article in the *Guardian Unlimited* tells of robbers shooting to death a policewoman in Great Britain and injuring her female partner. The article also tells of three other policewomen in Great Britain who have been killed in the line of duty.[10]

Of course, although we've talked in this chapter about policewomen being killed in the line of duty, we mustn't forget that now that policewomen work in the same jobs as policemen they're also susceptible to the same less-than-deadly dangers as policemen. For example, according to an article in *The Forensic Examiner,* "In terms of risk-by-profession, law enforcement officers had the highest rate of [non-fatal] victimization at 260.8 per 1,000."[11] This means that one out of every four police officers (including policewomen) is injured every year.

Although events such as those I've described in this chapter might make readers believe that women today would choose not to apply to become police officers, that isn't so. Although not in the same numbers as men, still many women today enter law enforcement regardless of the dangers. And, as we will see in the next chapter, once the gates had been opened for women in law enforcement, other public safety jobs, also previously male-only, additionally opened up for women. Once Liz and Betty had shown that women could do the job of police patrol as well as men, women began applying for and being accepted in many other public safety positions, such as firefighters, ambulance drivers, and medical technicians.

## 10

# WOMEN IN OTHER PUBLIC SAFETY JOBS

In 1973, Judith Livers' firefighter husband asked her to help him with his fire sciences class. She did, and while assisting him with his studies she became interested in firefighting herself. Consequently, not knowing the momentous step she was taking, Judith applied for a position with the Arlington County, Virginia, Fire Department (located just west of Washington, D.C.). The fire department accepted her and she began her career there in 1974.

Before this time there had been a number of women in the United States who had worked as volunteer firefighters, but these women didn't receive any pay or have to live at the firehouse as a part of their job. Also in 1973 the city of Winston-Salem, North Carolina, reportedly hired Sandra Forcier as a full-time police officer and an on-call firefighter (she became a full-time firefighter four years later). However, in 1974, when Judith Livers (later Brewer) began receiving a paycheck and, as a part of her job, living at a firehouse, she became the first full-time paid professional female firefighter in the United States.

Yet, like the first policewomen on street patrol, becoming the first full-time professional firefighter wasn't a smooth, trouble-free journey for Judith Livers Brewer. Judith's entry into the totally male-dominated field of firefighting turned out instead to be a road full of hazards. "The wives were upset about their husbands bunking with a woman," Judith told a reporter from the *Washington Post* in 1990.[1]

Since Judith was the first woman in professional fire service, the fire station the department assigned her to, Station No. 4 in Clarendon, naturally had no special facilities available for her. She slept in the same room as the men. Yet, while the men usually slept in their underwear, she slept in her clothes. Fortunately, she was able to use the private shower belonging to the battalion chief.

As Judith stated previously, many of the firefighters' wives didn't like her sleeping arrangement at all, and they demanded a meeting with the fire chief and the county manager. "The wives [were] extremely upset," Judith said. "One of them screamed at me and told me not to talk to her husband."[2] However, despite this opposition, Judith continued to stay at the firehouse.

And as if this conflict with the firefighters' wives wasn't a difficult enough way to start her career, Judith, once she realized the ground she was breaking, also knew that as the first female professional firefighter she would be watched in everything she did on the job. She quickly came to realize that every aspect of her work was going to be closely monitored and scrutinized, and that any failures on her part would be blown totally out of proportion. Fortunately, before applying to the fire department, Judith had exercised vigorously and built her strength up to the level necessary to do the job. Consequently, she found she could easily perform all the necessary functions of a firefighter.

Interestingly, much like Liz and Betty six years earlier, Judith didn't realize at the time she put in her application to become a firefighter that she would also become a trailblazer. "When she applied for the job she was not interested in breaking new ground as a woman," said a 2001 newspaper article about her. "Nor did she realize she would be the first. She just wanted to be a firefighter."[3]

The chief of the Arlington County Fire Department in 1974, Robert Groshon, much like Indianapolis Police Chief Winston Churchill, turned out to be a very forward-looking man, who could see that the wave of the future in firefighting would include women. By 1974, women had already established a hold in many police departments across the United States, and Chief Groshon obviously realized that firefighting would be next.

"I knew I was sticking my neck out," Chief Groshon said. "But there were no rules that said a woman couldn't be hired."[4] Yet, although the chief may have felt this way, many of the male firefighters at the Arlington County Fire Department obviously didn't. They signed a petition urging the chief not to hire any more women firefighters.

However, once Judith demonstrated that women could do the job of firefighting, other women across the country began to follow suit and join up at other fire departments. Judith Livers Brewer not only showed that women could be successful firefighters, but that they could also be leaders in fire service. When she retired in 1999, she held the rank of battalion chief.

As we have talked about in earlier chapters, Liz and Betty faced stern opposition when they first went out on street patrol as police officers. However, they eventually proved that women could do the job of police patrol just as well as men, which then opened the door for other policewomen in other cities. But in doing this, Liz and Betty also opened other doors. With women winning acceptance as patrol officers, the movement of women into firefighting became a natural progression, although, as we will see, like policewomen on street patrol, the first female firefighters faced stern opposition from many individuals who wanted to keep firefighting a male-only profession.

A major difference, though, for women applying for a police officer position as opposed to women applying for a firefighter position is that firefighting regularly requires a significant amount of physical strength and stamina in order to do the job. Consequently, those applying for a firefighter position will likely face a physical agility test at least as strenuous, and probably even more strenuous, than a police officer physical agility test. Also, a firefighter physical agility test will be more likely to be upheld by the courts because fire administrators can clearly show that it is job-relevant to have applicants drag heavy hoses, climb ladders, carry people from buildings, and so on. Therefore, a person who wants to become a firefighter must be prepared for a career that often requires considerable physical strength and stamina.

Although Judith Livers Brewer had gotten herself into top physical shape, and fortunately encountered a very forward-looking chief who saw no problem in hiring her, other fire chiefs across the country didn't feel the same. Many fire departments vigorously resisted hiring women, and in many of the departments only a court order forced them to open their application process to women.

The New York City Fire Department, for example, didn't begin hiring women until 1982. And it took a court case, *Berkman v. City of New York,* to at last force the fire department do this.[5] Brenda Berkman, who initiated this case and became the first woman hired by the New York City Fire Department, retired on September 14, 2006, with the rank of captain. Before her retirement, she had served as the commander of Engine House 239 in Brooklyn.

As we talked about in a previous chapter, even though today all large and medium-sized police departments hire policewomen on a regular basis, many small police departments in the United States have as of today still not hired any policewomen. Unfortunately, the same situation occurs in many small fire departments. Lanora Hackett, for example, a volunteer firefighter for the Vashon Island Fire Department in Washington state, won a lawsuit against the fire department in February 2009. She had applied for a paid position with the fire department and got top scores on the test, yet still the fire department passed her over for a lesser-qualified man. "They told me at that point that it was because I didn't fit in with the all-male culture," Hackett said.[6] The judge in her case ruled that the fire department had unlawfully discriminated against her. The court ordered that she be hired, and receive $150,000 and five years of back pay.

Not unexpectedly, since 1974 women in firefighting have faced many of the same problems that the first policewomen on street patrol faced. Many of the male firefighters didn't believe that women possessed the strength and stamina necessary to be a firefighter. It was a man's job and should stay that way. And unlike policemen, who had often had policewomen around the department for years before these women went out on street patrol, professional firefighters had never had women in their ranks or at their firehouses before 1974. Therefore, the intrusion of women into firefighting was near earth shaking for them.

To make matters worse, firefighters are usually required, as a part of their job, to sleep at the firehouse. When women first began joining fire departments, there were, of course, no separate facilities available for them, and so they often had to sleep in the same room as the men. As we saw in the Judith Livers Brewer case, this usually didn't make many of the firefighters' wives very happy. A study in 1995, for example, found that nearly half of all the fire departments contacted reported having received complaints from the spouses of male firefighters about the presence of female firefighters in the firehouse.[7]

Another significant detriment to being a female firefighter in the early years was that much of the gear firefighters wore had been designed exclusively for men. In the early years, female firefighters simply had to make do with the male firefighting equipment. And of course, firefighting being a totally male-dominated bastion for so many years, fire department administrators had never thought about developing a policy for pregnancy and in many cases didn't know what to do with pregnant firefighters.

Also, because firefighting was a totally male-dominated field for so many years, female firefighters, like female police officers, often suffered considerable sexual harassment on the job, and unfortunately many still do today. Some studies show that as many as 85 percent of female firefighters report that they have experienced sexual harassment.[8] And, because firefighters live and work together in very close quarters for prolonged periods, this sort of behavior is much more likely to occur in firefighting than in police work.

Yet, even with such a large amount of sexual harassment, like policewomen, only a small percentage of female firefighters ever officially report the incidents. Most don't want to make waves, many don't want to become known as whiners or troublemakers, and others fear that they'll face retaliation if they do report the sexual harassment.

This is not true for all female firefighters, however. Like a small percentage of female police officers, a small percentage of female firefighters sometimes decide not to just ignore the sexual harassment or to simply give up when fire administrators won't do anything about it. Some female firefighters have brought lawsuits against fire departments, and these cases have often cost fire departments millions of dollars.

In July 2007, for instance, a jury in California awarded a female fire-fighter on the Los Angeles Fire Department $6.2 million. She claimed, among other things, that male firefighters had put urine in her mouth-wash and made derogatory remarks to her. The city of Los Angeles also had to pay $1.7 million to a male firefighter that the fire department had retaliated against for supporting the female firefighter's claims.

A New Jersey female firefighter won a $450,000 verdict after success-fully proving sexual harassment, which included spreading rumors that she was sleeping with her supervisor. In New Haven, Connecticut, a jury awarded a female firefighter $1.5 million after it found that the fire department had engaged in intentional sexual harassment.

Captain Brenda Berkman, the first woman hired by the New York City Fire Department, also suffered serious harassment. She reported that she had the oxygen drained from her air tanks, received death threats on her answering machine, and that in the early years of her career most of the men at the firehouse wouldn't eat, talk, or train with her.

In the light of all these struggles and difficulties, how successful has the integration of women into firefighting been? According to the 2000 census, fire departments in the United States now employ more than 8,500 female firefighters. However, the report also stated that half of all the fire departments in the United States still do not have any female firefighters at all. On the other hand, some fire departments have hired a significant number of female firefighters. In Tuscaloosa, Alabama, for example, 24 percent of the firefighters are women; 23 percent in Kal-amazoo, Michigan; and 19 percent in Springfield, Illinois.[9]

Of course, once females broke the barrier into police patrol and firefighting, women naturally began looking into other pubic safety jobs that had also once been male-only domains. One of these jobs was emergency medical technician (EMT) or paramedic.

The first female EMT in the United States was reportedly a woman named Laurie Knop. According to her account,

> At the time I applied, there were only three paramedic schools in Los Angeles County. My first two attempts to enter paramedic school were unsuccessful—I didn't even get an application. But on the third and final try, I was granted the privilege to fill out an application at Queen's Para-medic School. To my great surprise, I was accepted.[10]

Yet, the road to becoming an EMT for Laurie Knop, not surprisingly, turned out to be a very bumpy one. "Dr. Lewis called [me later] to tell me he couldn't find an internship for me," she said in her diary. "Everyone had turned me down because of my sex."[11]

Still Laurie persevered. In February 1975, she graduated and became the first female EMT in the United States. However, before gaining employment in her chosen profession, she turned down several job offers because employers told her that she would be paid less than men in the same position. The prospective employers justified this by saying that they didn't think she could do as much as the men.

And like female police officers and firefighters, female EMTs often faced stern opposition from the men in this formally male-only profession. In a study reported in 1992, nearly half of the female EMTs surveyed said that they had experienced sexual harassment while on the job.[12]

Along with this opposition by the male EMTs, the public, as it did with female police officers and firefighters, also often had a difficult time accepting women as EMTs. At a National Emergency Medical Services Conference, participants heard of the case of a man who worried so much about the competency of two female EMTs that rather than be carried down some stairs on a stretcher by them, he scooted down the stairs on his buttocks, and then climbed onto the stretcher at the bottom.

The status of women, however, began to quickly change in the EMT field as more and more women entered it. The public and male EMTs, once they saw that women could perform the job as well as men, began to offer less resistance to the idea of female EMTs. Also, other members of the public safety field began seeing advantages to having female EMTs, and consequently supported their hiring. In sexual assault cases, for example, the victims, police officers found, often felt much more comfortable after being medically treated by a woman, and consequently could be interviewed by the police more quickly and easily.

In 1987, only twelve years after Laurie Knop found her first job as an EMT, the successful inclusion of women into the EMT field culminated in the election of Janet Head, a nurse and EMT, to the presidency of the National Association of Emergency Medical Technicians. This is a group composed of more than 27,000 EMTs. As further evidence of the acceptance of females in the EMT field, in a study conducted in

1996, 82 percent of the respondents, both male and female EMTs, told researchers that the sex of their partner didn't matter.[13]

In addition to becoming firefighters and EMTs, women also began moving into other, less visible public safety jobs, many of which had never before been held by women. Women began moving into jobs such as Emergency Management, Port Authority, Homeland Security, and others. In San Francisco, for example, Monique Moyer became the executive director of the Port of San Francisco in 2004. Part of her responsibility included the security of the port. In the same year, the mayor of San Francisco also appointed Annemarie Conroy as the Executive Director of Emergency Services and Homeland Security.

Finally, we spoke in chapter 9 about how New York City police officer Moira Smith gave her life trying to save others at the World Trade Center tragedy on September 11, 2001. Many people likely didn't know about Officer Smith, but probably even fewer people know that, along with Officer Smith, several other female public safety workers also lost their lives at the World Trade Center that day.

≪

Captain Kathy Mazza-Delosh of the Port Authority of New York and New Jersey Police sat in her Jersey City office on the morning of September 11. When she heard the report of the terrorist attack at the World Trade Center, she rushed out of her office and went straight to the scene. She immediately entered Tower One and began rescuing and evacuating people. Coming down from the twenty-ninth floor to the mezzanine level with a group of people she had rescued, Captain Mazza-Delosh found the exits blocked. Undeterred, she pulled out her revolver and shot out several glass windows, allowing the people to escape through them. She didn't leave with them though, but instead stayed inside to rescue more people. She died when the tower collapsed. "She wouldn't have left until everyone was helped out," Kathy's mother said. "That's the kind of person she was—always there helping others."[14]

≪

Yamel Merino, a twenty-four-year-old EMT, part of a two-person ambulance team, also rushed to the World Trade Center upon hearing of the attack. An order came from the command post set up at the scene that one member of each ambulance team was to stay with the ambulance, while the other member was to go into the buildings to rescue people. Yamel didn't hesitate. She went into Tower One and began getting the people out. She also died when the tower collapsed. "She worked any time, anywhere," said Al Kim, director of MetroCare Ambulance Group, where Yamel worked. "She was the first wave. She was ready to go."[15]

≫

Also, although few people realized it because of all the gear they wear, many of the firefighters at the World Trade Center tragedy were women. Paula Zahn of *CNN News* interviewed Captain Brenda Berkman, who also responded immediately to the scene, about the number of female rescue workers at the World Trade Center tragedy.

"It's impossible to know, Paula, because, you know, once we put on our gear and our work clothes we look just like the guys," Captain Berkman said. "But I would say that over the course of the next several weeks, though, there were literally hundreds of women who responded to that site. There were over half of all the women firefighters . . . down there on 9/11."[16]

In the preceding chapters, we have looked at how, starting in 1968, policewomen began moving out of their designated safe jobs within police departments and started moving into all areas of police work. In chapter 11, we will look at how women stand today in police service, and whether all of the problems we have talked about so far have been resolved or are still present.

# ⓫

# POLICEWOMEN TODAY
# AND TOMORROW

In 1973, Beverly Harvard and her husband, who worked then at Delta Airlines, were talking with a male friend about the city of Atlanta's aggressive recruitment of policewomen to patrol the streets. During the conversation, Beverly told the two men that she thought she could probably be a good police officer. The friend laughed and said no way.

"It was 1973, and my husband, Jimmy, and a friend of his were talking about how the women who might be suited to be police officers had to be 6 foot 2 inches tall, weigh 200 pounds and have deep voices," Beverly recalled.[1] Irritated at the friend's response, Beverly again said that she thought she would make a good police officer, and afterward turned to her husband for support, expecting him to say, "My wife, she can do anything," and go on with the conversation. "But," Beverly recalls, "he said, 'Yeah, you're right, she could never be a police officer.'"[2] This response incensed Beverly, and so to prove her point she bet her husband $100 that she could apply and be accepted at the Atlanta Police Department. He took the bet.

Beverly had just graduated from Morris Brown College with a degree in sociology, and with these credentials she went to apply to join the Atlanta Police Department. She filled out an application and then began two months of rigorous testing; eventually she passed all of the entrance exams. Following this, to her husband's surprise, the Atlanta Police Department accepted her into the next recruit class.

Now that Beverly had won the bet, her husband, after paying off, began to worry about the danger of his wife becoming a police officer. They talked it over, and finally Beverly proposed that she stay at the training academy only long enough to learn a bit about the police department, get some information about Constitutional Law, and perhaps pick up some self-defense tips. All of this, she said, would be helpful later when she moved on to another career field. Beverly's plan sounded reasonable, and so her husband agreed to a short stint at the training academy.

However, as I talked about in an earlier chapter, police work can be both intoxicating and addictive. Beverly Harvard found it to be very much so. Consequently, by the time she was halfway through the training academy, Beverly had fallen in love with police work.

"At some point, prior to finishing that academy," Beverly said, "you would have thought I entered knowing and wanting to be a police officer. I did a total conversion during training. I was ready."[3] So, instead of leaving as she had planned and going on to another career, Beverly decided to stay as a policewoman at the Atlanta Police Department.

Her first assignment, however, a 6 p.m. to 2 a.m. walking beat in a high-crime area, upset her husband so much he couldn't stop worrying about her. He became so distressed that he even began shadowing her in his car as she walked her beat. Knowing what it would do to her career if someone found out what her husband was doing, Beverly had several discussions with him, and finally he accepted the fact that she was a thoroughly trained police officer, who could take care of herself.

In the following years, Beverly began to advance upward within the ranks of the Atlanta Police Department. Finally, in October 1994, twenty years after Beverly's first walking-beat assignment, Bill Campbell, the mayor of Atlanta, appointed her as the new chief of police. She would command a police department of more than two thousand officers, and control an annual budget of $93 million.

☰

Birmingham, Alabama, during the turbulent years of the civil rights movement, stood out as one of the epicenters of racial intolerance. The police of Birmingham in those days would often let loose police dogs and fire hoses on civil rights protesters. In addition, the Ku Klux Klan regularly terrorized the city's black residents.

In 1980, a black woman named Annetta Watts (later Nunn) joined the Birmingham Police Department. She rose rapidly through the ranks to become a sergeant in 1983, a lieutenant in 1991, a captain in 1995, and a deputy chief in 2000. Her upward progression in the police department didn't surprise anyone who really knew her. Her father, a coal miner, and her mother, a nurse, already knew their daughter was special by the time she spoke as the valedictorian of her high school graduating class. She then went on to college, where she majored in criminal justice, and graduated *magna cum laude.* Following college, she joined the Birmingham Police Department at a time when they had begun to heavily recruit minorities. However, she didn't want or seek any special treatment because she was black or a woman. "When I took the job, I told people to judge me by my character, not by the color of my skin or by my sex," she told a reporter for the *New York Times.*[4]

In 2003, the mayor of Birmingham appointed Annetta Watts Nunn, a black woman, as the chief of police. This was the same police department that forty years earlier had been notorious for its mistreatment of black citizens. She would oversee a police department of 1,100 officers and an annual budget of $70 million.

≫

On January 2, 2007, Cathy L. Lanier took the oath of office as the chief of police of the 3,800-member Washington, D.C., Police Department. Before being named chief of police, she had served as a uniformed district commander; commander of the Narcotics Branch; and head of the Special Operations Division, which included Homeland Security, Counter-Terrorism, and a number of specialized units such as the Emergency Response Team, mounted patrol, canine, and others.

≫

The mayor of Cleveland, Ohio, in 2001 swore in Mary Bounds as the new chief of police. In 2004, Mayor Gavin Newsom of San Francisco chose Heather Fong to be his new chief of police. In 2006, Kim Crannis took over as the chief of police of Blacksburg, Virginia. In 2007, Elizabeth Bondurant became the chief of police of Plainsboro, New Jersey. Also in 2007, the mayor of Orlando, Florida, appointed Val Demings to be the next chief of police. In 2008, Henderson, Nevada, a suburb of Las Vegas, welcomed Jutta Chambers as their new chief of police. In 2009, Margaret Ackley began her term of service as the chief of police of New London, Connecticut.

What all of these anecdotes are meant to illustrate is how very far women in law enforcement have come in just a little over forty years since Liz and Betty first went out on street patrol in Car 47. Policewomen have advanced from virulent opposition in the 1960s to resigned acceptance a decade or two later, and then from being no longer an unusual sight in the 1990s to chief executives today.

In addition, however, to becoming chiefs of police, a number of women in the last forty years have also advanced to other top executive jobs within law enforcement. Because the climb of these women has been so spectacular in the very short time during which women have had the opportunity to advance within police departments, I want to spend a few minutes giving some examples of this leap forward by women in law enforcement.

For example, we have seen before in this book how in the 1970s and 1980s many of the Los Angeles policemen aggressively opposed policewomen in male jobs. But in June 2000, Chief of Police Bernard C. Parks of the Los Angeles Police Department promoted Margaret Ann York to Deputy Chief. "This is the greatest time ever for women in police service," Deputy Chief York said. "Opportunities to work interesting and challenging assignments are open to all. Women have become true partners in police service."[5]

As another example, in 1971, Bonni G. Tischler joined the U.S. Customs Service as a sky marshal. The U.S. Customs Service in 1971 became the first federal agency to hire women as full-fledged police officers. Prior to this time, regulations prohibited women in federal service from carrying firearms. It finally took an Executive Order to change this. In 2001, thirty years after beginning work as a sky marshal, Bonni assumed the title of Assistant Commissioner for the Office of Field Operations at the U.S. Customs Service. In this position, she supervises 7,500 employees. "We have a complex mission that includes enforcing over 600 laws for about 40 different agencies," Bonni said of her job.[6]

Marilyn Diaz joined the Pasadena Police Department in 1974, and became their first policewoman on street patrol. In those days, she had to use the bathroom to change into her uniform because the police department had no women's locker room. She also faced stiff resistance from the male officers in the department. What kept her going was some advice she received from Robert McGowan, the chief of police at that time. "He said that my success would have a large impact on how women who were to follow me were to be accepted," Marilyn recalls.[7] In March 2006, Marilyn left the Pasadena Police Department to become chief of police of the Sierra Madre Police Department. When she left Pasadena, she was the commander of their Patrol Division and responsible for 160 officers.

Sonoma County, California, just north of San Francisco, is known for its wine industry. In 2007 it made news of another sort. Captain Linda Suvoy of the Sonoma County Sheriff's Department received a promotion to the rank of Assistant Sheriff. In her new capacity she oversees the operation of Sonoma County's two jails, and also supervised a $200 million construction project that will double the bed space in the jails. "Detention facilities are complex," Assistant Sheriff Suvoy said. "You're running a city, basically."[8]

Another example of female advancement in law enforcement occurred when United States Attorney Joseph P. Russoniello in April 2008 announced the appointment of Annemarie Conroy as the new Law Enforcement Coordinator for the U.S. Attorney's Office, Northern District of California. We talked earlier in this book about Annemarie Conroy, whom the mayor of San Francisco appointed as the Executive Director of Emergency Services and Homeland Security for the city of San Francisco. "I am delighted Annemarie Conroy has joined our team," said Russoniello. "She brings to our office her extensive knowledge of local and regional government derived from over a decade of working in San Francisco and the Bay Area."[9]

Karin Montejo retired after spending thirty years at the Miami-Dade Police Department. During her time there she served as the head of the Domestic Crimes Bureau, as a District Uniformed Commander, as a lieutenant in the Homicide Bureau, and finally retired as the chief of Miami-Dade's Administration and Technology Bureau. While serving as a police officer she also earned a Ph.D. in Corporate and Organizational Management, and now heads up Montejo Consulting, Inc.

As we have spoken about several times in this book, the rest of the world often mirrors the United States in regard to policewomen. This also applies to how far policewomen have advanced in the last few decades. For example, in June 2008, Norma Graham, of Scotland, received a promotion to Chief Constable of Fife Constabulary. Before this, she had been the Assistant Chief Constable of the Central Scotland Police. She had also previously held the position of Detective Chief Superintendent in charge of the Criminal Investigations Division (CID). In her newest position, she will head a force of more than one thousand officers. "She is highly qualified having worked at a senior level for a number of years and has fantastic experience," said Peter Grant, the leader of Fife Council.[10]

As I have shown so far in this chapter, women have made tremendous strides in law enforcement during the last forty-plus years. Women have attained goals in policing that were unthinkable not that long ago. However, I don't want readers to believe that, because of the major advances made by some women in law enforcement, all of the problems these women faced getting there are now gone, because they're not.

Because we're discussing in this chapter the subject of policewomen today and tomorrow, in order to be balanced we must look not just at the great achievements made, but also at some of the problems that still remain. We must recognize that, even with all of the great advances, pockets of resistance to policewomen still exist, that policewomen today still face some hurdles and roadblocks in their struggle for equality, and that they will likely continue to face them tomorrow. Consequently, there still remain some areas of law enforcement that need improvement. For example, although there are almost two hundred female police chiefs across the nation, this is still only about 1 percent of all the chief of police positions in the United States.

In addition, each year, the FBI gathers crime statistics from police departments all across the nation and puts them into a book called *Crime in the United States* (also known as the *Uniform Crime Reports* [UCR]). This book then details how many robberies, burglaries, murders, and so on occurred in the United States. However, also included in this publication is information about the makeup of police departments across the nation. In its 2008 edition, the UCR reported that of all the police personnel in its reporting law enforcement agencies, which totaled about 700,000 police officers, only 11.7 percent were female. The statistics gathered in the UCR also showed that the police departments with the largest percentage of policewomen, 18.3 percent, were in cities with populations of more than one million people. The police departments with the smallest percentage of policewomen, 7.4 percent, turned out to be in nonmetropolitan counties. Sadly, the report also showed that many small police departments in the United States have never had any female police officers at all.[11]

Of course, these percentages are just overall statistics for the entire United States. Individual police departments, naturally, can vary. For example, we talked earlier in this book about how only 2.6 percent of West Virginia's state troopers are female. In Connecticut, on the other hand, 7 percent of the state troopers are female. Statistics show the national average of female state troopers to be 6.5 percent. Sadly, in addition to the low number of West Virginia state troopers, in West Virginia's ten largest cities, only 4.6 percent of the officers are women, whereas the state's sheriff's departments average only 2.2 percent.[12]

As another example, a look at the police departments in just one state, Iowa, shows very clearly how many police departments in the United States have resisted hiring policewomen. Out of the 235 Iowa police departments listed in the 2008 UCR, 60 percent of them do not have any female officers at all.[13]

An article in the February 2009 issue of *Police Chief* magazine stated, "An analysis of the UCR data showed that most of the police agencies reporting to the FBI did not employ any policewomen in 2003."[14] On a positive note, federal agencies, which had no female police officers at all prior to the 1970s, are well above the national average, with the combined federal agencies having an average of 15 percent female officers.

Another roadblock for female officers, as we talked about in a previous chapter, is that many of the police departments in the United States still require their applicants to pass a strenuous physical agility test. This is true even though, unlike fire departments, these tests have never been proven to accurately reflect the job of a police officer.

Again, as I've said several times in this book, I do think that new female police officers should be fit and strong. I just don't think we should force them to meet the same fitness and strength standards as men. Physiologically, this is not practical or fair. But in truth, some police departments don't really care about being practical or fair, because their physical agility tests are not meant to be real tests, but simply a subterfuge to keep women out of police departments. In support of this position, a study conducted by the National Center for Women & Policing found that police departments without these strenuous physical agility tests have 45 percent more policewomen than agencies that do have them.[15]

Along with physical agility testing, we also talked at some length earlier about the opposition of many of the rank and file policemen to women in law enforcement. In addition, we also spent considerable time discussing the resulting sexual harassment of women who became police officers despite this opposition. Have the passing years and the advancement of policewomen finally cured these two problems? Sadly, only partly. Although there is no longer any widespread rank and file opposition to female police officers, still some small pockets of resistance remain. And even though many police departments, after paying out or witnessing other police department pay out millions of dollars for sexual harassment lawsuits, have established strict policies against sexual harassment, still small pockets of this problem also remain. As anyone who watches the news knows, policewomen still file sexual harassment lawsuits every year. There is obviously work yet to be done by some police administrators across the United States. Former Chief of Police Penny Harrington told me:

> As more and more women joined the police department, it became readily apparent that women could do the jobs that had once been male-only just as well as the men could. But this did not change the mythical belief in female incompetency held by many of the male officers. I had hoped

that as the years passed, that attitude would die out—but it has not. There is still a hardcore group of men in most police agencies that do not believe women should be police officers. There are still lawsuits being filed by women who are subjected to horrendous sexual harassment and sex discrimination. And the sad part of all of this is that it is the public who suffers. Women do bring different experiences and talents to law enforcement. We are half of the population and we are as brave and capable as our brother officers. I hope there comes a day when not a thought is given to the gender of the police officers of this country.[16]

We have also talked quite a bit in this book about the relegation of policewomen to certain "female" jobs within a police department. Has this problem finally disappeared in the twenty-first century? Regrettably, no. There are still some police departments that attempt to maintain this pre-1970s practice. One policewoman told a researcher:

I have watched our agency expand from an all white male organization in 1973 to the over 2000 member agency it is today. In spite of this, a 1950s style of thinking remains pervasive. Law enforcement is historically slow to evolve and our agency is no exception. In 2007, women still have a "place," illustrated by the large concentration of females in "nurturing" assignments (sex crimes, victim advocacy, juvenile crime prevention) and support assignments (human resources, data maintenance, communications, executive assistants). Women are excluded from the line-level assignments carrying the highest potential for future advancement (like SWAT teams) and rarely included in policy decisions for the agency.[17]

But unfortunately, as two policewomen explain in the following text, it is not always just the male establishment in police departments that cause this stereotyping of policewomen to certain "female jobs." Occasionally, policewomen themselves help to continue this practice. Sergeant Jody Kasper told me:

There are many challenges to working as a minority in a non-traditional job, some obvious and some much more subtle. I think one of the biggest problems for female officers is facing the daily task of challenging social norms and expectations about what women can and should do. It seems that women have been accepted into policing with some expectations that have proven difficult to shake, and the blame falls on both men and women. Women officers today still find themselves, as I did, working sexual assault investigations, handling family violence cases, working in community service units, or as DARE officers. Male officers tend to lean more toward SWAT teams, drug units, violent crime investigations, etc. As far as I can see, these stereotypes still exist in policing today.[18]

Former Chief Karin Montejo of the Miami-Dade Police Department also weighed in on this problem:

At one time there were a lot of women who liked the idea of being on a police department, but didn't like police work, so they would take administrative jobs. Then we got in a group of very dedicated women who wanted to do the job of a police officer. They knew this meant being available 24-7, that it meant missing birthdays and other family functions, but they wanted the job and that was just part of it.

While we still get a number of these excellent female officers joining police departments every year, I've also seen a slight swing recently back to females joining up because they see police work as a good job with good benefits, if they can just get through the academy and their probation. Then they look for that administrative assignment, but still want the recognition, respect, and benefits of being a road officer, yet want no part of that job. I think we're going to lose a lot of the tremendous strides and progress we've made over the last thirty to forty years, because for some new women it's not their career, it's a job with benefits.[19]

Regardless of the roadblocks, problems, and obstacles that remain in the twenty-first century, an article published in 1989 in the journal *Public Personnel Management* said that, "A noted authority on women in law enforcement predicts that within a few decades 50 percent of all police officers will be women, and that women will hold 30 percent of all law enforcement administrative posts."[20] This is an interesting and very optimistic prediction for the future. However, as I said earlier, when we look at policewomen today and tomorrow, we must not only look at the great strides and advances policewomen have made, and how much further they will likely advance in the future, but we must also look realistically at some of the problems the future will hold. One of these problems, I believe, will be the recruitment of women into law enforcement.

Consequently, although I do believe that police departments should do all they can to hire more women and make the police departments of tomorrow much more representative of the communities they serve, I don't know if a 50-50 split is a realistic objective for the foreseeable future. This is particularly true because the percentage of policewomen almost a decade into the twenty-first century still only stands at about 12 percent. Part of the reason for this low percentage, of course, has to do with physical agility tests, and so on; another part of the reason has to do with how women look at the job of being a police officer. So, while I want readers to know I support the hiring of policewomen, I don't want them to think that I look at the subject with such fervor that I'm not able to be objective about the realities of the job.

I experienced one of these realities when I served six years as head of the Indianapolis Police Department's Personnel Branch, the duties of which naturally included recruiting. What I found was that we simply couldn't get near as large a pool of female applicants as we could male applicants. Regularly, we would have several thousand men apply for a class of forty to fifty recruits, but seldom would we get as many as two hundred women to apply. And although readers might think that this sounds like a lot of female applicants, it really wasn't because we also always found that a large number of these women couldn't pass the testing and background investigation.

One of the reasons, I believe, for this smaller number of female applicants is that police work is a job that simply doesn't appeal to some women. There are many reasons for this lack of appeal, including irregular hours, department policies that are not family-friendly, and women's fear that they will be relegated to "female" jobs. In addition, the job also often involves dealing with the absolute worst of society in squalid conditions, and occasionally there is some very real danger involved. Many women (and some men, for that matter) don't find these agreeable conditions for a career. I don't want readers to think that I'm putting down women, because I'm certainly not. I am simply reflecting on what I believe the future holds based on what I saw in our recruiting efforts and on what I found through my conversations with many prospective female recruits. Of course, I also want readers to know that this is not just my opinion. The officers cited in the following text agree.

"It takes a certain woman to do this job," said Officer Amy Evertson of the Saratoga Springs, New York, Police Department. "You have to really want to get into law enforcement, and not a lot of women are comfortable with it."[21]

"I have been in law enforcement for over 25 years, and it still surprises me that more young adults do not see law enforcement as a viable career, especially women," said Chief Betsy Hard of the Bloomfield, Connecticut, Police Department.[22]

"The job of recruiting and keeping women with a department is a challenge across the nation," said Lieutenant Terry Gabbert of the Owensboro, Kentucky, Police Department, which is seeking to increase its complement of female officers. "The pool of women interested in police work is already small, and finding women who can pass the physical tests, polygraph test, criminal background check, and psychological testing is difficult."[23]

From my own experience, and from all of the interviews I've done with policewomen and possible policewomen recruits, the biggest of all the problems discussed so far, and, as a result, the biggest drawback to police work for women (and many men for that matter) is the irregular hours. Police officers often have to work shifts that conflict with a woman's desire to have both a career and family. Being a police officer often means missing important family functions, such as birthdays and school programs, which can be especially difficult when children are little. Consequently, many women either don't join police departments or leave for more family-friendly jobs once they decide to have children.

"I would love to have more women in law enforcement," said San Jose Police Chief William Lansdowne in a 2002 newspaper article, "and we work hard to increase the numbers. But our research says it's not recruitment that's the problem—it's retention."[24] San Jose is experiencing what many police departments across the United States are experiencing today: policewomen leaving for other jobs so they can spend more time with their families. "I loved being in law enforcement," said former San Jose police officer Stephanie Reinhardt, "yet I wanted to be a mother and I wanted to be there for my children, and it was hard to do that given the hours over at the police department."[25] Consequently, after spending four years as a police officer, Stephanie left and took a non–law enforcement job with day shift hours and weekends off.

Because of the many policewomen leaving law enforcement in order to spend more time with their families, many police administrators across the country have begun aggressive recruitment programs to attract more women to replace them. Police recruiters now routinely visit women's colleges, job fairs for women, and other locations where they can make contact with possible female applicants. And some states, such as Pennsylvania, have gone so far as to set up mobile recruiting offices in motor homes in order to travel to these places. "It's critical for our Department's work force to reflect the diverse nature of the communities we serve," said Colonel Jeffrey B. Miller, Pennsylvania State Police Commissioner.[26]

Yet even though I don't realistically see any time in the near future when police departments will be 50 percent women, and even though there still remain a number of problems in law enforcement that can make it a less desirable career option for some women, I want to end this chapter on a positive note, because I truly believe that the future for policewomen is positive. I want readers to know that I see many signs that tell me the role of policewomen in law enforcement will continue in the upward mode it has been moving in since 1968.

Two of the positive signs I see are that the movement of women into all specialty areas of police work continues to grow, and that policewomen also continue their rise within the rank structure of police departments. When I conducted my research for this book, there were no areas of police work where I wasn't able to find at least some women now involved. Doors closed in the past have now been opened. In addition, I have also given many examples in this and the preceding chapters of policewomen who have risen through the ranks to become top law enforcement executives.

Along with the movement of policewomen into all areas and ranks of police departments, there are other positive signs that show policewomen are no longer just considered modified policemen, but are rather a force of their own. A good example of this is the change in police uniforms for women. The outfits of Liz and Betty aside, when most policewomen first began street patrol across the United States in the 1970s, they were forced to wear uniforms and equipment meant for men. Because of the differences in male and female physiology, often the slacks, gun belts, holsters, and so forth didn't fit women correctly, making them difficult to use and many times raising serious safety concerns, such as difficulty getting the gun out of the holster. Today, however, most police uniform manufacturers have a separate line of uniforms just for policewomen.

"As the women were joining the forces they felt a lot of discrimination because of the fact that they were different," said Andrew Foss, director of marketing for Elbeco, a uniform manufacturing company. "One of the places they saw that discrimination was every day when they put on this uniform that didn't fit, and it caused resentment."[27] Today, as I said earlier, most uniform manufacturers, including Elbeco, have a line of police uniforms specifically for women.

In addition to uniforms, when police officers first began wearing soft body armor, most of it was again designed for men. This is also no longer the case. An article on ballistic vest manufacturing stated:

> To best meet women's needs, some companies have assembled panels of female officers to find out directly from them what they want and what best fits their bodies, while still providing the protection they require on the street. For example, PT Armor put together a panel about five years ago to develop a more comfortable, streamlined stitching design that cuts down on bulk.[28]

As a further sign of many people's belief in the value and permanence of policewomen, when I was conducting research for this book I came across a number of schools and training courses designed specifically to help policewomen advance their careers. Some of these courses included Advanced Female Officer Survival, Pistol Training for Policewomen, and Effective Law Enforcement Problem Solving for Policewomen.

Finally, a clear sign of the importance and permanence of policewomen in the twenty-first century is that, in 2007, the U.S. State Department began a recruitment process for policewomen to take part in international police missions. An article about this initiative stated, "Research indicates that the inclusion of women in police units improves internal dynamics and performance, decreases the incidence of excessive force, and encourages community-oriented policing, emphasizing crime prevention over crime control."[29]

This statement is one that is today embraced by many administrators of police departments all across the nation. These administrators have come to realize that adding policewomen to their agencies greatly improves the functioning of their departments, and significantly reduces the number of complaints from citizens. Consequently, many police departments have begun advertising programs, using the Internet and other outlets, to show women that they are wanted and needed on their police departments. These types of publicity campaigns are important because many women have often not given much thought to a career in law enforcement, or believe law enforcement is a field they won't be welcomed in. And once police departments can persuade women to join, police administrators know that these women will then often become valuable recruiters themselves because they usually love the job and will tell other women about it. Retired Sergeant Betsy Brantner Smith, of the Naperville, Illinois, Police Department, told me:

> My 29-year career in law enforcement has been much like a love affair, with all of the thrills, heartbreaks, exhilaration, desperation, tears, laughter, and with the crazy intensity that raw, gut-wrenching human emotion offers. It was rarely the citizens or co-workers I had a problem with, but management could be fickle. Sometimes I was the favorite, sometimes I was hated; sometimes I was a painful thorn in someone's side. But being a female cop taught me how to survive, and how to teach others to thrive in this profession that is really a calling, not just a career.[30]

Sergeant Jody Kasper told me:

> I am incredibly fortunate to work in a progressive community that emphasizes equality and social justice. We have a woman mayor, District Attorney, and women working in other prominent positions. In my time with the Northampton Police Department, I have certainly experienced sexism, but it has not overshadowed my career. I have been granted every special assignment I have put in for, was selected for the Detective Bureau ahead of my male peers, and was promoted to sergeant ahead of my male peers. In that respect, I don't feel that being a woman has significantly impaired my career, and I am quite happy with my department and with my peers.[31]

As proof of the widespread nature of this female satisfaction with police work, in 2008, a study reported in the *Justice Policy Journal* measured job satisfaction among both male and female police officers. What the study discovered was that most policemen and policewomen love their job. According to the study, "The results of these measures indicate a high level of job satisfaction in general. Nearly 85 percent of the respondents were pleased with their jobs overall." The study then goes on to say, "The results for both male and female officers were consistent across all measures." [32]

I think most readers will have to agree that 85 percent of employees pleased with their jobs is a huge number. This says a lot about how policewomen have not only become accepted in police departments, but also have now become such an integral part of their departments that they no longer see law enforcement as a dead-end job. Rather, most policewomen see it as a career in which not only can they help others but in which they can also feel totally fulfilled themselves.

# SOME FINAL THOUGHTS

Liz told me:

> Betty and I, when we first went out in Car 47, didn't talk about or even
> think about making any great contributions to history. We just wanted to
> be police officers. We also didn't give much thought to what we were do-
> ing for the feminist movement; we just wanted to show everyone that we
> could do the job of police officer, regardless of our gender. As it turned
> out, this attitude proved to be our best weapon in gaining acceptance by
> the men.[1]

Liz was absolutely correct in her analysis. I firmly believe that if she
and Betty had gone out on a crusade, loudly demanding that they be accepted as equals, insisting that it was their right, the acceptance would
likely never have happened. But rather than demanding their due, Liz
and Betty instead went out and demonstrated to the male officers that
they could do the job of street patrol as well as a man, and that was what
eventually broke the gender barrier.

We have seen this attitude in action throughout this book. Policewomen who have successfully moved into high ranks and into previously
male-only jobs did it not by demanding that they be there as equals,
but rather by demonstrating that they deserved to be there. This is the

only way to gain true acceptance. Betsy Gelardi, when interviewing for the job of chief of police of Dobbs Ferry, New York, in 2008, told the interview panel, "This is not about being male or female. Those days are long gone. We're all cops. Since Day 1 I've done everything that every man on this force has done. . . . I've gone into bar fights, I've worked the midnight shifts."[2]

Today, more than forty years after Liz and Betty rolled out in Car 47, policewomen still don't have a free ride in their careers, but their progression through police departments is certainly not as arduous as before. As two noted authorities on women in policing stated:

> Yet, despite the pessimistic views of some regarding the future of police-women, there is much to be optimistic about during the early years of the 21st century. A number of legal and cultural obstacles to women in policing have been removed. There are signs that things are beginning to improve, and that women considering a career in law enforcement today may not have to experience all the hardships that confronted their predecessors.[3]

I believe this statement is very true. Again, women don't have a free ride in law enforcement, but if they enter the profession and work hard at it, they can attain any goals they may set. For example, when I was commander of the Homicide Branch, I witnessed policewomen whose goal it was to become top-notch homicide investigators. And when I gave them the chance, most succeeded in their goal. I saw the same in all of the other commands I held during my career. Police work today is a field ripe for women who want to have a career that is fulfilling on many levels. "Law enforcement is still a non-traditional field of work for women," said Professor of Criminal Justice Michael Carpenter, "but just like men, they realize that it is a sound profession that offers a challenging career."[4]

Yet, along with being a challenging career that gives its practitioners a feeling of deep fulfillment from doing a job that means something, from doing a job that makes a difference in many people's lives, police work is something more. It is a fellowship of individuals, a family of people all dedicated to helping others and serving the community. When you work closely day after day with others in dangerous and often highly emotional situations, a strong, family-like bond develops. This bond is what keeps many men and women in law enforcement even though they could do better financially in other fields. It's what keeps them there when others want them to leave.

Chief Deputy Dave Stafford of the Raleigh County, West Virginia, Sheriff's Department said it best, "I would not stereotype the law enforcement profession as specifically male. It's just not that way. I think in law enforcement, in general, it doesn't matter if you're male, female, city, county, state—we're all seen as a family. We are all connected by the badge we wear."[5]

I was very fortunate to have spent my thirty-eight-year career as a police officer during a time when I could witness the very beginnings of policewomen on street patrol up to what I saw when I left law enforcement in 2007: almost total acceptance of policewomen as an integral part of law enforcement. Even with all the problems that remain, I think the future will only become better for women seeking a career in law enforcement. I think that most of the women who enter police work today and in the future will not see the huge barriers that policewomen of the past did, but instead will see a near-level playing field on which their careers can be played out on an equal basis with all others.

The End

# APPENDIX

## Remembering Liz
*Patrol Officer Melanie G. Snow (ret.)*

I first met Elizabeth Coffal in April 1983 (or so I thought). I was on uniform patrol then and broke my foot chasing a suspect who had just stabbed another man in a bar fight. Liz was in charge of the Property Recovery Unit, and, because of my injury, the police department assigned me to her unit on light duty until my foot healed. I liked the assignment because her unit eventually became legendary, recovering so much stolen property that the police department didn't have room to store it all. At that time I didn't know anything about Liz being one of the first two policewomen in the United States to be assigned to street patrol. Unfortunately, the instructors at the training academy didn't include any mention of it during our training. I just thought she was a great person, and we became friends immediately. Liz wasn't into bragging, so it wasn't until years later that I found out about her accomplishments.

Once assigned to her unit, I talked with Liz and found that we had gone to the same grade school and high school, and even grew up in the same neighborhood. As we continued to talk, I found that, rather than 1983, I had actually first met Liz fifteen years before. She and her partner, Betty Blankenship, had taken a stolen vehicle report at my home when I was in high school back in 1968. I recalled the two women coming to our house, and how sharp they had looked in their uniforms. My sister, who was twelve at the time, bombarded them with questions about police work and about how soon she could apply to become a policewoman. While I was certainly impressed with their demeanor and how professional they looked, I believed police work wasn't for me. I had made plans then to join the military after high school and become a nurse. As it turned out though, my sister joined the army and became a nurse, while I became a cop.

A short time after my foot healed and I returned to my regular assignment on street patrol, Liz's husband, Major Robert Robinson, contacted me about working in his office as the Special Events Officer. In this job I would coordinate the police involvement in large events in Indianapolis, which included conventions, parades, the 500 Mile Race, and the like. Since this was a straight day shift job and I had two small children, I accepted his offer. Naturally, this job helped Liz and I continue our friendship. In addition, my husband, a captain at that time, worked closely with Liz's husband, and so off-duty the four of us would often go to dinner and a movie, or just go out for drinks and talk.

My favorite memories of Liz, though, were the things she and I did together. We enrolled in classes at the Indianapolis campus of Indiana University/Purdue University, and we even took sewing classes together. Liz, a very talented seamstress, made most of her own clothing, sewed sports jackets for her husband, and even made wedding gowns and bridesmaid's dresses for her nieces. Liz also decorated cakes, and once made a three-tiered wedding cake for one of her nieces. After retirement, Liz tried her hand at painting and did a number of excellent portraits.

But along with being a very multitalented individual and a great friend, Liz also was a person I knew I could count on anytime I needed to. Once when my children were at Liz's house swimming, our daughter jumped off the diving board and hit her lip on the edge, cutting it pretty severely and needing stitches. This was before cell phones, so Liz couldn't reach me or my husband. Fearing that if she waited the cut might scar, Liz took our daughter to the hospital and told them that she was her mother and then signed for the treatment. When my husband and I got to the hospital we couldn't go back to see our daughter because the hospital staff told us that her mother was already back there with her. Our daughter's lip healed without a scar, and Liz and I often laughed about this later.

While of course I eventually learned about Liz's contribution to the advancement of policewomen and all of the awards and accolades she received from across the country, I had to prod her to get her to talk about those days. Liz and I often laughed when she told stories about how she and Betty had worn skirts, high heels, and carried their guns in their purses. She told me stories of them having to hike up their skirts and kick off their shoes when they chased suspects, and about all the pairs of hose they ruined.

Because of our close friendship that allowed me to get Liz to open up, I could compare how different things were for today's policewomen compared to what they were in 1968. Even in 1980, when I joined the police department, we still had some male officers who felt that policewomen shouldn't be on street patrol. And occasionally even I, later in my career, when in a dangerous situation or out in nasty weather, would think sarcastically, "Thanks a lot, Liz. I could be sitting behind a desk in a nice warm office." But in actuality, all policewomen everywhere are indebted to Liz and Betty. Because of them, policewomen everywhere now have the same opportunities as the men. We make the same pay and can work in any job in the police department. It's truly a debt we all owe them.

In November 1996, after Liz and her husband had been retired for several years from the Indianapolis Police Department, a doctor diagnosed her husband with lung cancer. He passed away in January 1998. Liz was naturally devastated. I knew she missed him desperately and I tried to do all I could to cheer her up. Fortunately, she eventually ran into an old friend she had worked with years before, who had lost his wife to cancer several years earlier. At first they were just friends, then three years later they married.

However, only a few years after Liz's marriage, her doctor found a spot on her left lung. They decided to just wait and see if the spot changed. Two years later, the spot had grown and needed to come out. During testing, the doctors found that Liz now had thyroid cancer, which had to be treated first before attending to the spot on her lung. By the time she did receive treatment for her lung it had become cancerous, and the malignancy had spread to her lymph nodes, eventually also turning up in her hip and liver. Liz knew it was too late to save her. Despite this, she agreed to take part in some very painful research studies because she wanted to help others beat cancer even though she knew she couldn't.

On April 8, 2009, Liz passed away. I delivered her eulogy and it was one of the hardest things I will ever have to do. Along with being a friend for more than twenty-six years, she was also a truly amazing woman who never saw herself as anyone special, just someone who wanted to be a cop. The world, I feel, is a lesser place without her.

# NOTES

## CHAPTER 1

1. Interview by author, 6 July 2007.
2. Interview by author, 6 July 2007.
3. The President's Commission on Law Enforcement and the Administration of Justice, *The Challenge of Crime in a Free Society* (Washington, D.C.: U.S. Government Printing Office, 1967), 125.
4. Interview by author, 12 November 2007.
5. Interview by author, 12 November 2007.
6. Interview by author, 12 November 2007.
7. Interview by author, 12 November 2007.
8. Interview by author, 12 November 2007.
9. Interview by author, 12 November 2007.

## CHAPTER 2

1. "A Policewoman on Trial," *Survey Graphic*, 15 April 1922, www.sameshield.com/press/sspress13.html (accessed 26 May 2008).
2. "A Policewoman on Trial."
3. "A Policewoman on Trial."

4. "She Still Insists on Policewomen," *New York Times*, 31 March 1907, www.sameshield.com/press/sspress01a.html (accessed 26 May 2008).

5. Barbara Albiston, "Crime Fighting 'Mothers,'" *Bulletin*, March 2001, 3.

6. "Police Matrons," *Harper's Weekly*, August 1890, www.sameshield.com/press/sspress01.html (accessed 26 May 2008).

7. Peter Horne, "Policewomen: Their First Century and the New Era," *Police Chief*, September 2006, 23–32.

8. Bertha H. Smith, "The Policewoman," *Good Housekeeping*, March 1911, 22–25.

9. "Women in the LAPD," LAPDonline, 2008, www.lapdonline.org/history_of_the_lapd/content_basic_view/833 (accessed 12 June 2008).

10. "Famous Policewoman Urges Prevention of Crime," *New York Times*, 22 December 1912, 13 (SM).

11. August Vollmer, "Meet the Lady Cop," *Survey Graphic*, 15 March 1930, www.sameshield.com/press/sspress104.html (accessed 26 May 2008).

12. "Today in San Francisco History," *Sfist*, 2008, http://sfist.com/2008/12/09/today_in_san_francisco_history_miss.php (accessed 11 March 2009).

13. "Girls and Khaki," *Survey Graphic*, 1 December 1917, www.sameshield.com/press/sspress09c.html (accessed 26 May 2008).

14. James Walter Smith, "Enter the Lady Cops of Gotham," *Boston Evening Transcript*, 18 May 1918, www.sameshield.com/press/sspress09aa.html (accessed 26 May 2008).

15. Smith, "The Policewoman."

16. "Women in the LAPD."

17. August Vollmer, "The Policewomen and Pre-Delinquency," *Woman Citizen*, March 1926, www.sameshield.com/press/sspress34.html (accessed 26 May 2008).

18. Vollmer, "Meet the Lady Cop."

19. O. W. Wilson, *Police Administration* (Columbus, OH: McGraw-Hill, 1963), 290, 334.

20. Edith Abbott, "Training for the Policewoman's Job," *Woman Citizen*, April 1926, www.sameshield.com/press/sspress35.html (accessed 26 May 2008).

21. "The Effective Policewoman: A Study Program," *Woman's Journal*, May 1931, www.sameshield.com/press/sspress107.html (accessed 26 May 2008).

22. Helen D. Pigeon, "Policewomen and Public Recreation," *The American City*, October 1927, www.sameshield.com/press/sspress128.html (accessed 26 May 2008).

23. Josephine Nelson, "On the Policewoman's Beat," *Independent Woman*, May 1936, www.sameshield.com/press/sspress112.html (accessed 26 May 2008).

24. "Women Police of Detroit," *New York Times*, 13 March 1921, 4(sec 9).

25. Susan L. Miller, *Gender and Community Policing: Walking the Talk* (Lebanon, NH: Northeastern University Press, 1999), 82.

26. Kerry Segrave, *Policewomen: A History* (Jefferson, NC: McFarland & Company, 1995), 45.

27. Mina C. Van Winkle, "The Policewoman," *Survey Graphic*, 24 September 1924, www.sameshield.com/press/sspress21.html (accessed 26 May 2008).

28. Eleanor Hutzel, "The Policewoman," *The Annals of the American Academy of Political and Social Science*, November 1929, www.sameshield.com/press/sspress119.html (accessed 26 May 2008).

29. Louis Brownlow, "The Policewoman's Sphere," *National Municipal Review*, March 1928, www.sameshield.com/press/sspress106.html (accessed 26 May 2008).

30. Eleanor Hutzel, "The Policewoman's Role in Social Protection," *Journal of Social Hygiene*, December 1944, www.sameshield.com/press/sspress126.html (accessed 26 May 2008).

31. "Women Become Policemen as Police Become Soldiers," *American City*, April 1943, www.sameshield.com/press/sspress118.html (accessed 26 May 2008).

32. Alec Waugh, "Women in Policing" (paper presented at the Australian Institute of Criminology Conference, Sydney, Australia, 29 July 1996), 2.

33. Felicia Shpritzer, "A Case for the Promotion of Policewomen in the City of New York," *Journal of Criminal Law, Criminology, and Police Science* 50, no. 4 (November–December 1959), 415–19.

## CHAPTER 3

1. Interview by author, 29 March 2009.

2. Interview by author, 6 July 2007.

3. Interview by author, 28 April 2009.

4. Derrick Stokes, "Police Protection Is a Relative Matter," *Indianapolis News*, 18 March 1991, 1(C).

5. Julie N. Lynem, "Female Officers Make Strides in Police Work," *Indianapolis Star*, 27 October 1996, 1(A).

6. Interview by author, 28 April 2009.

7. Interview by author, 28 April 2009.

8. Interview by author, 17 June 2009.

9. Amy Rabideau Silvers, "Estrada Blazed Trail for Other Officers," *Milwaukee Journal Sentinel*, 25 August 2006.

10. Keith Herbert, "Malverne Welcomes First Female Police Officer," *Newsday*, 11 July 2007.

11. Denisse Salazar, "Pepper Spray and Endless Pushups Is What It Took," *Orange County Register*, 3 April 2008.

12. Interview by author, 17 June 2009.

13. John Penney, "Q & A with Donna Ash Brown, Putnam's First Female Police Officer," *Norwich Bulletin*, 10 December 2008.

14. "Dothan's First Female Officer Retires," *4WTVY*, 21 December 2006, www.wtvynews4.com/home/headlines/4985226.html (accessed 17 March 2009).

15. Interview by author, 27 July 2009.

16. Muriel L. Whetstone, "The Nation's First Black Woman Sheriff: Jackie Barrett," *Ebony*, August 1995.

17. Renee Alfieri, "Human Relations Internship with the New York City Police Department," *Empowering Inquiry*, 2008, www.empoweringinquiry .com/nypd3.html (accessed 18 March 2009).

## CHAPTER 4

1. Interview by author, 7 December 2007.

2. Thomas R. Keating, "Policewomen Manning Patrol Car," *Indianapolis Star*, 11 September 1968.

3. "Women on Patrol?" *Indianapolis News*, 16 September 1968.

4. Interview by author, 6 July 2007.

5. Craig Beardsley, "Women in Law Enforcement," *Indianapolis Magazine*, April 1976, 37–43.

6. Bettie Fruits, "Women 'Cops' Launch Squad Car Duty," *Indianapolis News*, 13 September 1968.

7. Interview by author, 6 July 2007.

8. Interview by author, 6 July 2007.

9. Nick Stanhouse, "From Desk to Patrol Car," *The Indiana Trooper*, August 1979, 41–43, 225–29.

10. Joe Fahy, "Pioneer Policewoman to Retire," *Indianapolis News*, 29 April 1989, 1(C).

11. Fruits, "Women 'Cops' Launch Squad Car Duty."

12. Interview by author, 6 July 2007.

13. Beardsley, "Women in Law Enforcement," 37.

14. Susan Lennis, "Guys Will Ride in Car 47 Anytime . . . Cause the Fuzz Are Feminine," *Indianapolis Star Magazine*, 27 June 1971, 7–11.

15. Fahy, "Pioneer Policewoman to Retire."

16. Lennis, "Guys Will Ride in Car 47 Anytime," 8.
17. Letter dated 12 October 1970.
18. Interview by author, 6 July 2007.
19. Stanhouse, "From Desk to Patrol Car," 42.
20. "Policewomen Manning Patrol Car," *Police Journal*, Fall 1968, 37.
21. Interview by author, 6 July 2007.
22. Interview by author, 6 July 2007.
23. Interview by author, 6 July 2007.
24. Interview by author, 22 January 2008.
25. Interview by author, 28 April 2009.

## CHAPTER 5

1. Mark Alesia, "Patrick on Win: Women 'Capable of Anything,'" *Indianapolis Star*, 22 April 2008, 1(A).
2. Interview by author, 7 December 2007.
3. Interview by author, 15 June 2009.
4. Interview by author, 15 June 2009.
5. Interview by author, 23 June 2009.
6. Michelle Caruso, "Fuhrman Led 'Klan' vs. Female Officers on Tapes, O.J. Trial Cop Tells of 'Tribunals,'" *New York Daily News*, 28 April 1997.
7. Mary Ellen Gale, "Calling in the Girl Scouts: Feminist Legal Theory and Police Misconduct," *Loyola of Los Angeles Law Review* 34, no. 1 (2001): 691–747.
8. Robert Scheer, "Joseph Wambaugh: What LAPD Needs Is Women to Combat Testosterone Level," *Los Angeles Times*, 14 July 1991, 3(M).
9. Albert Ross Jr., "Female Officers Are Rare Sight in Area's Police Departments," *Augusta Chronicle*, 2 June 2003, http://chronicle.augusta.com/stories/060203/met_070-8069.000.shtml (accessed 17 March 2009).
10. Interview by author, 23 June 2009.
11. Letter dated 12 October 1970.
12. Chandra Niles Folsom, "Women Advancing in Police Work, But Few Pursue It," *PoliceApp.com*, April 2008, www.policeapp.com/JusticeJournal/NewsView.asp?NewsId=16 (accessed 18 March 2009).
13. Chelsea Kellner, "Female Officers Put Up Long Fight for Acceptance," *Associated Press*, 11 March 2009.
14. Interview by author, 23 June 2009.
15. "Female Officers in Knoxville Are Ordered to Cut Their Hair," *New York Times*, 26 October 1981, 13(A).

16. Caryn Tamber, "Philly's First Female Cops Fought an Uphill Battle for Equality," *Daily Pennsylvanian*, 28 November 2000, http://thedp.com/node/21868 (accessed 27 May 2008).

17. Natalie Canavor, "Being One of the Guys Is Not a Chief Concern for One of Nassau County's First Policewomen," *Long Island Business News*, 9 June 2006.

18. Chelsea Kellner, "Wilmington's First Female Cop Put Up Long Fight for Acceptance," *StarNewsOnLine*, 8 March 2009, www.starnewsonline.com/article/20090308/ARTICLES/903072970?Title=Wilmington-s-first-female-cop-put-up-long-fight-for-acceptance (accessed 15 August 2009).

19. Adam C. Eisenberg, "The First Nine—Lure of Equal Pay Changed SPD Culture Forever," *Seattle Post Intelligencer/Seattle Times*, 28 October 2001, 4(D).

20. Interview by author, 6 July 2007.

21. Interview by author, 6 July 2007.

22. Interview by author, 28 April 2009.

23. Peter B. Hoffman and Edward R. Hickey, "Use of Force by Female Police Officers," *Journal of Criminal Justice* 33, no. 2 (2005): 145–51.

24. Peter Horne, *Women in Law Enforcement* (Springfield, IL: Thomas, 1980), 71.

25. Andy Newman, "Town Rejects Female Officer," *New York Times*, 28 February 1997, 1(B).

26. Kelly Keith and Charlotte Kratchmer, "Train Women Separately from Men," *Law and Order*, June 2007, www.hendonpub.com/resources/article archive/details.aspx?ID=1291 (accessed 12 March 2009).

27. Ruth C. Wamuyu, "Three Female Officers Work for UPD," *Spartan Daily*, 26 October 2004, www.sjsupd.com/pages/news/102604.html (accessed 18 March 2009).

28. Melanie Basich, "Female Police Officers Must Walk a Fine Line between Fitting In and Making Their Own Way in Law Enforcement," *Police*, June 2008, www.policemag.com/Articles/2008/06/Women-Warriors-1.aspx (accessed 12 March 2009).

29. Interview by author, 15 June 2009.

30. Susan Aaron, "Women with Badges," *FastWeb*, 2009, www.fastweb.com/resources/articles/index/110245 (accessed 17 March 2009).

31. Susan E. Martin, *Doing Justice, Doing Gender* (Thousand Oaks, CA: Sage, 2006), 73.

32. Eisenberg, "The First Nine."

33. Michelle Malkin, "What's Wrong with This Picture?" michellemalkin.com, 12 March 2005, http://michellemalkin.com/2005/03/12/whats-wrong-with-this-picture/ (accessed 26 April 2009).

34. Ann Coulter, "Freeze! I Just Had My Nails Done!" anncoulter.com, 16 March 2005, www.anncoulter.com/cgi-local/article.cgi?article=46 (accessed 7 June 2009).

35. Jarka Halkova, "Policewomen Seem to Be Winning the Fight for Respect," *Czech Radio*, 8 December 2005, www.radio.cz/en/article/73525 (accessed 11 March 2009).

36. "Female Mounties Don't Feel Respected, Poll Finds," *RCMP Watch*, 29 October 2007, www.rcmpwatch.com/female-mounties-dont-feel-respected-poll-finds/ (accessed 17 March 2009).

37. Keith Foster, "Gender and Excessive Force Complaints," *Law and Order*, August 2006, www.hendonpub.com/resources/articlearchive/details.aspx?ID=764 (accessed 12 March 2009).

38. "Men, Women, and Excessive Force," The National Center for Women & Policing, April 2002, www.womenandpolicing.org/PDF/2002_Excessive_Force.pdf (accessed 12 March 2009).

39. "Men, Women, and Excessive Force," April 2002.

40. Peter B. Bloch and Deborah Anderson, *Policewomen on Patrol: Final Report* (Washington, D.C.: Police Foundation, 1974), 2.

41. Brent Steel and Nicholas Lovrich, "Equality and Efficiency Tradeoffs in Affirmative Action—Real or Imagined?" *Social Science Journal* 24, no. 1 (1987): 53–70.

42. Foster, "Gender and Excessive Force Complaints."

43. Interview by author, 23 June 2009.

44. Susan Edmiston, "Policewomen: How Well Are They Doing a Man's Job?" *Ladies Home Journal*, April 1975, 126.

45. Polly Horne, "A Comparison of the Attitudes of Male Police Officers toward Female Police Officers from 1976 to 1994," 1996, www.fdle.state.fl.us/Content/getdoc/a68d0fd7-2cb3-4236-a378-81005626dd34/horne2.aspx (accessed 13 March 2009).

46. Kristen Leger, "Public Perceptions of Female Police Officers on Patrol," *American Journal of Criminal Justice* 21, no. 2 (March 1997): 231–49.

## CHAPTER 6

1. *McNamara v. City of Chicago*, 853 F.2d 572.

2. *Dothard v. Rawlinson*, 433 U.S. 321, 97 S.Ct. 2720.

3. Penny E. Harrington and Kimberley Lonsway, "Equality Denied: The Status of Women in Policing: 2000," The National Center for Women & Policing, Beverly Hills, CA, 2000, 3.

4. Harrington, "Equality Denied," 5.

5. Adam T. Rossi, "Progress of Female Officers," *Saratoga Today*, 29 February 2008, www.saratoga.com/today/2008/02/progress-of-female-officers.html (accessed 12 March 2009).

6. Iliana Limon, "Victory a Hollow One for Female Officer," *Albuquerque Tribune*, 26 November 2002, 1(A).

7. Mandalit del Barco, "L.A. SWAT Unit on Verge of Accepting First Woman," *National Public Radio*, 14 June 2005, www.npr.org/templates/story/story.php?storyId=90015810 (accessed 3 May 2009).

8. "Justice Department Sues Mississippi City Alleging Discrimination against a Female Lieutenant," U.S. Justice Department Press Release, 16 October 1996.

9. Karin Montejo, "Success Factors of Women Who Have Achieved Positions of Command in Law Enforcement" (Ph.D. diss., Lynn University, Boca Raton, FL, 2008).

10. The National Center for Women & Policing, *Recruiting & Retaining Women: A Self-Assessment Guide for Law Enforcement* (Los Angeles: The National Center for Women & Policing, 2000), 26, 94, 133.

11. "Female Officers Win Suit against Nassau Police," WCBSTV, 17 November 2008, http://wcbstv.com/topstories/gener.discrimination.nassau.2.867074.html (accessed 18 March 2009).

12. Emelyn Cruz Lat, "Female Officers Furious at Firemen," *Seattle Times*, 25 April 1996.

13. Interview by author, 23 June 2009.

14. *Adams v. Nolan*, 962 F.2d 791.

15. *UAW v. Johnson Controls, Inc.*, 499 U.S.187 (1991).

16. Stephanie Ebbert, "Under Hillman, Troopers Alleged Bias," *Boston Globe*, 9 March 2006.

17. "$1M Awarded in Alleged LAPD Sexual Favors Case," KNBC, 3 October 2007, www.knbc.com/print/14265190/detail.html (accessed 4 Oct. 2007).

18. Joseph Ax, "Teaneck Settles Suits for $4.9M," NorthJersey.com, 30 April 2009, www.northjersey.com/ews/crimeandcourts/Teaneck_settles_suits_for_49M.html (accessed 4 May 2009).

## CHAPTER 7

1. "Portland Blacks Outraged by 'Sleeper-Hold' T-Shirts," *Eugene Register-Guard*, 30 April 1985, 5(A).

2. Tom Wicker, "Police Troubles Know No Gender," *Spokesman-Review*, 2 May 1985, 4(A).

3. "LAPD Working to Get More Female Officers," *Los Angeles Times*, 30 May 2003, www.sameshield.com/news/lapd.html (accessed 18 March 2009).

4. Keith Foster, "Gender and Excessive Force Complaints," *Law and Order*, August 2006, www.hendonpub.com/resources/articlearchive/details .aspx?ID=764 (accessed 12 March 2009).

5. "Justice Department Announces Court Decision that Eire, Pennsylvania Police Officer Test Discriminates against Women," U.S. Justice Department Press Release, 14 December 2005.

6. *Dothard v. Rawlinson*, 433 U.S. 321, 97 S.Ct. 2720.

7. *Thomas v. City of Evanston*, 610 F.Supp. 422, 431 (N.D. Ill. 1985).

8. Larry T. Hoover, "Trends in Police Physical Ability Selection Testing," *Public Personnel Management* 21, no. 1 (1992): 29–40.

9. David E. Terpstra and R. Bryan Kethley, "Organizations' Relative Degree of Exposure to Selection Discrimination Litigation," *Public Personnel Management* 31, no. 3 (2002): 277–92.

10. John Gales Sauls, "Proving Business Necessity: The Disparate Impact Challenge," *Lectlaw*, April 1995, www.lectlaw.com/files/emp35.htm (accessed 8 May 2009).

11. "Tearing Down the Wall," National Center for Women & Policing, Spring 2003, www.pennyharrington.com/impactofagility.htm (accessed 7 May 2009).

12. *Lanning v. SEPTA*, 308 F.3d 286.

13. "Hiring and Retaining More Women," National Center for Women & Policing, Spring 2003, www.womenandpolicing.org/pdf/NewAdvantagesReport .pdf (accessed 17 March 2009).

14. Interview by author, 17 June 2009.

15. Susan E. Martin, "Women on the Move?" *Police Foundation Reports*, May 1989, 2.

16. Brian A. Reaves, "Local Police Departments 1993," U.S. Department of Justice—Bureau of Justice Statistics, NCJ-148822, April 1996, iii.

17. Venessa Garcia, "'Difference' in the Police Department," *Journal of Contemporary Criminal Justice* 19, no. 3 (August 2003): 330–44.

18. Peter Horne, "Policewomen: Their First Century and the New Era," *Police Chief*, September 2006, 23–32.

19. Amelia A. Pridemore, "Percentage of W. Va. Female Police Officers in Single Digits," *Register-Herald*, 24 January 2009, www.register-herald.com/ local/local_story_024232858.html (accessed 13 March 2009).

20. "Federal Law Enforcement Officers, 2002," U.S. Department of Justice—Bureau of Justice Statistics, NCJ-199995, August 2003, 7.

21. Takesha Pettus, "Three Officers, Including First Female, Join SRPD," *Sentinel* (New Jersey), 26 July 2000, 1(A).

22. Susan McMahon, "Pelham's First Female Officer Welcomes Challenge," *Lowell Sun Online*, 28 June 2001, www.uml.edu/Media/News%20Articles/article124.html (accessed 16 March 2009).

23. Keith Herbert, "Malverne Welcomes First Female Police Officer," *Newsday*, 11 July 2007.

24. John J. Shaughnessy, "Policewomen Chalk Up String of Firsts," *Indianapolis Star*, 1 August 1982, 1(B).

25. Albert Ross Jr., "Female Officers Are Rare Sight in Area's Police Departments," *Augusta Chronicle*, 2 June 2003, http://chronicle.augusta.com/stories/060203/met_070-8069.000.shtml (accessed 17 March 2009).

26. Robert L. Snow, *SWAT Teams: Explosive Face-Offs with America's Deadliest Criminals* (New York: Perseus, 1999).

27. Andrea King, "SWAT Graduates First Female Officer," *Journal* (Michigan), 14 September 2006, www.journalgroup.com/Belleville/1123/swat-graduates-first-female-officer (accessed 16 March 2009).

28. Tomas C. Mijares, "Selecting Police Personnel for Tactical Assignments: Considerations for Female Officers," *Applied H.R.M. Research* 4, no. 2 (1993): 94–101.

29. Mijares, "Selecting Police Personnel," 99.

30. Susan Edmiston, "Policewomen: How Well Are They Doing a Man's Job?" *Ladies Home Journal*, April 1975, 126.

31. Muriel L. Whetstone, "The Nation's First Black Woman Sheriff: Jackie Barrett," *Ebony*, August 1995.

32. Jodi Helmer, "Blazing the Trail," *Nervy Girl*, September/October 2002, www.sameshield.com/press/sspress129.html (accessed 26 May 2008).

## CHAPTER 8

1. Erin Bryce, "North Port Remembers Michele," *Sarasota Herald Tribune*, 15 July 2006, 8(B).

2. Interview by author, 22 January 2008.

3. Lyda Longa, "Female Cops Love Their Careers," *News-Journal*, 1 March 2009, www.news-journalonline.com/NewsJournalOnline/News/Local/new-EAST02030109.htm (accessed 17 March 2009).

4. Karin Montejo, "Success Factors of Women Who Have Achieved Positions of Command in Law Enforcement" (Ph.D. diss., Lynn University, Boca Raton, FL, 2008).

5. Montejo, "Success Factors of Women."

6. Susan Grant, "Dating a Female Cop," Officer.com, 8 July 2008, www.officer.com/publication/printer.jsp?id=29618 (accessed 16 March 2009).

7. B. Thompson, A. Kirk-Brown, and A. Brown, "Police Women and Their Partners: Influence and Outcomes of Work Stress in the Family" (paper presented at the Australasian Conference of Women and Policing, Brisbane, Australia, July 1999), 5.

8. Thompson, Kirk-Brown, and Brown, "Police Women and Their Partners," 4.

9. Interview by author, 23 June 2009.

10. Susan Grant, "When Cops Marry Cops," Officer.com, 8 July 2008, www.officer.com/publication/printer.jsp?id=32856 (accessed 25 May 2009).

11. Chelsea Kellner, "Female Officers Put up Long Fight for Acceptance," *Associated Press*, 11 March 2009.

12. Susan Edmiston, "Policewomen: How Well Are They Doing a Man's Job?" *Ladies Home Journal*, April 1975, 126.

13. "Hiring and Retaining More Women," National Center for Women & Policing, Spring 2003, www.womenandpolicing.org/pdf/NewAdvantagesReport.pdf (accessed 17 March 2009).

14. Gina Gallo, "A Family Affair," *Police*, February 2005, 36–40.

15. Gallo, "A Family Affair," 38.

16. "How Male, Female Police Officers Manage Stress May Accentuate Stress on the Job," *Medical News Today*, 28 February 2009, www.medicalnewstoday.com/articles/140610.php (accessed 12 March 2009).

17. Melanie Basich, "Female Police Officers Must Walk a Fine Line Between Fitting In and Making Their Own Way in Law Enforcement," *Police*, June 2008, www.policemag.com/Articles/2008/06/Women-Warriors-1.aspx (accessed 12 March 2009).

18. Aaron Besecker, "Stress Seen Hitting Female Police Most," *Buffalo News*, 29 December 2008, www.buffalonews.com/cityregion/story/534938.html (accessed 17 March 2009).

19. Kim Quaile Hill and Michael Clawson, "The Health Hazards of Street Level Bureaucracy: Mortality among the Police," *Journal of Police Science* 16, no. 4 (1988): 243–48.

20. Thomas E. Baker and Jane P. Baker, "Preventing Police Suicide," *FBI Law Enforcement Bulletin*, October 1996, 24–27.

21. Michelle Perin, "So, You Want to Date a Female Cop?" Officer.com, 10 March 2009, www.officer.com/web/online/Police-Life/So-You-Want-to-Date-a-Female-Cop/17$45721 (accessed 16 March 2009).

22. Perin, "So, You Want to Date a Female Cop?"

23. Grant, "Dating a Female Cop."

24. Jim Herron Zamora, "Study Finds Cops Twice as Likely to Abuse Family," *San Francisco Examiner*, 17 November 1997, 1(A).

25. Deepa Kandaswamy, "Indian Policewomen Practice Policing and Politicking," *Ms.*, Winter 2004.

26. Jarka Halkova, "Policewomen Seem to Be Winning the Fight for Acceptance," *Czech Radio*, 8 December 2005, www.radio.cz/en/article/73525 (accessed 11 March 2009).

27. "My Son Hates the Idea of Me Becoming a Policewoman," Gardenweb.com, 13 December 2001, http://ths.gardenweb.com/forums/load/parents/msg1212231629555.html (accessed 3 December 2009).

28. Interview by author, 7 December 2007.

29. Derrick Stokes, "Police Protection Is a Relative Matter," *Indianapolis News*, 18 March 1991, 1(C).

30. "10 Most Dangerous Jobs in America," *Publications International*, March 2009, http://money.howstuffworks.com/10-most-dangerous-jobs-in-america.htm (accessed 24 May 2009).

## CHAPTER 9

1. "Policewoman Mourned," *Indianapolis News*, 25 September 1974, 4.

2. Marilyn Schnepp, "My Friend Shanty," *Faith Writers*, 16 August 2006, www.faithwriters.com/article-details.php?id=49572 (accessed 20 June 2008).

3. John C. Cawdrey, "Constance E. (Connie) Worland," *The Backup: Newsletter of the California Reserve Peace Officers Association*, Summer 2006, 2.

4. "No Charges to Be Filed in F.B.I. Agent's Death," *New York Times*, 12 October 1985.

5. "Policewoman Moira Smith," *Scottish Daily Record*, 11 September 2002, www.womenatgroundzero.com/Pages/GlasgowRecord.html (accessed 20 May 2008).

6. Sean Gardiner, "Moira Ann Smith," *Newsday*, 13 February 2002, http://cf.newsday.com/911/victimsearch.cfm?id=423 (accessed 20 June 2008).

7. Leslie Eaton, "Officer's Slaying Leaves New Orleans Asking Why," *New York Times*, 31 January 2008, www.nytimes.com/2008/01/31/us/31shooting.html (accessed 20 May 2008).

8. Michael Kunzelman, "Hundreds Mourn Slain Policewoman," WWLTV.com, 1 February 2008, www.wwltv.com/local/stories/wwl020108tpmourners.7d5b2876.html# (accessed 6 September 2009).

9. Allen Johnson Jr., "The Legacy of Officer Cotton," *New Orleans Magazine*, 1 April 2008, www.neworleansmagazine.com/a/news/the-legacy-of-officer-cotton (accessed 20 May 2008).

10. "Female Police Officer Shot Dead," *Guardian Unlimited*, 19 November 2005.

11. "Officer Down: Characteristics of Cop Killings," *The Forensic Examiner*, 22 March 2008.

## CHAPTER 10

1. Stephanie Griffith, "Few Women Follow Virginia's Trailblazing Firefighter," *Washington Post*, 25 December 1990, 1(PC).

2. "First Female Firefighter," *Arlington Fire Journal*, 18 March 2005, http://arlingtonfirejournal.blogspot.com/2005/03/first-female-firefighter.html (accessed 25 March 2009).

3. Ingrid Kauffman, "Profile: Judith Brewer," *Arlington Sun Gazette*, 18 January 2001.

4. "First Female Firefighter."

5. *Berkman v. City of New York*, 672 F.2d 899.

6. Owen Lei, "Female Firefighter Wins Suit against Vashon Island FD," *King 5 News*, 12 February 2009, www.king5.com/news/local/60054812.html (accessed 1 June 2009).

7. Karen Barber, Kathy Miller, and Ellen Rosell, "Firefighting Women and Sexual Harassment," *Public Personnel Management* 24, no. 3 (1995): 339–50.

8. "Sexual Harassment in the Fire Service," International Association of Women in Fire & Emergency Services, 2008, www.i-women.org/issues.php?issue=3 (accessed 15 March 2009).

9. "United States Census 2000," www.census.gov/main/www/cen2000.html (accessed 27 February 2009).

10. Laurie Knop, "Woman Paramedic Pioneer," *Emergency* 7 (1977): 39–43.

11. Knop, "Woman Paramedic Pioneer."

12. Kate Dernocoeur and James N. Eastman, "Have We Really Come a Long Way? Women in EMS Survey Results," *Journal of Emergency Medical Services* 17 (1992): 18–19.

13. Sheryl Gonsoulin and C. Eddie Palmer, "Gender Issues and Partner Preferences among a Sample of Emergency Medical Technicians," *Prehospital and Disaster Medicine* 13, no. 1 (1997): 41–47.

14. Kathy Magrini, "Town Holding Street Dedication to Honor Captain Kathy Mazza-Delosh," *Massapequa Post*, 9 October 2002, 1(A).

15. "Living Tribute to Yamel Merino," *Living Tributes*, 2009, http://living tributes.com/livingtribute.php?memid=836 (accessed 2 June 2009).

16. "American Morning with Paula Zahn," CNN.com, 21 February 2002, http://transcripts.cnn.com/TRANSCRIPTS/0202/21/ltm.06.html (accessed 1 June 2009).

## CHAPTER 11

1. Ronald Smothers, "At Work with: Beverly Harvard," *New York Times*, 30 November 1994, 1(C).

2. Muriel L. Whetstone, "Atlanta's Top Cop—Police Chief Beverly J. Harvard," *Ebony*, March 1995, 92–95.

3. Whetstone, "Atlanta's Top Cop," 93.

4. David M. Halbfinger, "A Black Woman Sits in Bull Connor's Seat," *New York Times*, 3 May 2003, 12(A).

5. "First Female Officer Promoted to Deputy Chief," *Los Angeles Police Beat* 46, no. 7, July 2000, 1.

6. "Profiles of Leadership: Bonni G. Tischler," *The Business of Government*, Spring 2001, www.sameshield.com/press/sspress124.html (accessed 26 May 2008).

7. Cynthia H. Cho, "Policewoman Breaks the Brass Ceiling," *Los Angeles Times*, 28 March 2006, http://articles.latimes.com/2006/mar/28/local/me-chief28 (accessed 11 March 2008).

8. Katy Hillenmeyer, "Top Female Officer to Oversee Jail Expansion," *Press Democrat*, 5 June 2007, 1(A).

9. "United States Attorney Joseph P. Russoniello Announces Appointment of Annemarie Conroy as Law Enforcement Coordinator," U.S. Justice Department Press Release, 24 April 2008.

10. Michael Howie, "Scotland's First Woman Chief Constable to Lead Fife Force," *The Scotsman*, 7 June 2008, http://news.scotsman.com/lawand order/Scotland39s-first-woman-chief-constable.4162254.jp (accessed 21 August 2009).

11. "Uniform Crime Reports," www.fbi.gov/ucr/ucr.htm (accessed 29 June 2009).

12. Amelia A. Pridemore, "Percentage of W.Va. Female Police Officers in Single Digits," *Register-Herald*, 24 January 2009, www.register-herald.com/local/local_story_ 024232858.html (accessed 13 March 2009).

13. "Number of Full-Time Law Enforcement Employees by Agency as of October 31, 2007," www.dps.state.ia.us/commis/ucr/2007/2007_UCR_Table_LE.pdf (accessed 29 June 2009).

14. Peter Horne, "Policewomen: Their First Century and the New Era," *Police Chief*, September 2006, 23–32.

15. Susan E. Martin, *Doing Justice, Doing Gender* (Thousand Oaks, CA: Sage, 2006).

16. Interview by author, 15 June 2009.

17. Karin Montejo, "Success Factors of Women Who Have Achieved Positions of Command in Law Enforcement" (Ph.D. diss., Lynn University, Boca Raton, FL, 2008).

18. Interview by author, 15 June 2009.

19. Interview by author, 23 June 2009.

20. Brent S. Steel and Rebecca L. Warner, "Affirmative Action in Times of Fiscal Stress and Changing Value Priorities: The Case of Women in Policing," *Public Personnel Management* 18 (Fall 1989): 291–309.

21. Adam T. Rossi, "Progress of Female Officers," *Saratoga Today*, 29 February 2008, www.saratoga.com/today/2008/02/progress-of-female-officers.html (accessed 12 March 2009).

22. Chandra Niles Folsom, "Women Advancing in Police Work, But Few Pursue It," PoliceApp.com, April 2008, www.policeapp.com/JusticeJournal/NewsView.asp?NewsId=16 (accessed 18 March 2009).

23. Justin Willis, "Owensboro, Ky., Police Department Seeks to Increase Number of Female Officers," *Messenger-Inquirer*, 2 February 2003.

24. "San Jose Police Struggle to Recruit, Retain Female Officers," *Mercury News*, 29 May 2002.

25. "San Jose Police Struggle to Recruit."

26. "Pennsylvania Governor Rendell Announces New, Customized State Police Mobile Recruiting Office," press release from the Office of the Governor of Pennsylvania, 5 June 2003.

27. Alex Roman, "Female Police Officers Are a Minority and Their Uniform Needs Have Largely Been Ignored by the Market; but that's Changing," *Police*, December 2005, www.policemag.com/Print/Articles/2005/12/The-Other-10-Percent.aspx (accessed 12 March 2009).

28. Melanie Hamilton, "Ballistic Vest Manufacturers Are Finding New Ways to Meet Female Officers' Needs," *Police*, October 2007, 31–36.

29. "Department of State Seeks to Recruit Police Women for International Civilian Police Mission," Department of State Media Note, 29 June 2007.

30. Interview by author, 26 July 2009.

31. Interview by author, 15 June 2009.

32. William Sousa and Jane Florence Gauthier, "Gender Diversity in Officers' Evaluations of Police Work," *Justice Policy Journal* 5, no. 1, Spring 2008, www.cjcj.org/files/gender_diversity.pdf (accessed 26 May 2009).

## SOME FINAL THOUGHTS

1. Interview by author, 12 February 2008.

2. Jacqueline Mroz, "Female Police Chiefs, a Novelty No More," *New York Times*, 6 April 2008.

3. Penny E. Harrington and Kimberly Lonsway, "Current Barriers and Future Promise for Women in Policing," in *The Criminal Justice System and Women*, 3rd ed., eds. Barbara R. Price and Natalie J. Sokoloff (New York: McGraw-Hill, 2004), 495–510.

4. Adam T. Rossi, "Progress of Female Officers," *Saratoga Today*, 29 February 2008, www.saratoga.com/today/2008/02/progress-of-female-officers.html (accessed 12 March 2009).

5. Amelia A. Pridemore, "Percentage of W.Va. Female Police Officers in Single Digits," *Register-Herald*, 24 January 2009, www.register-herald.com/local/local_story_024232858.html (accessed 13 March 2009).

# BIBLIOGRAPHY

"10 Most Dangerous Jobs in America." *Publications International,* March 2009. http://money.howstuffworks.com/10-most-dangerous-jobs-in-america .htm (accessed 24 May 2009).

"$1M Awarded in Alleged LAPD Sexual Favors Case. KNBC. 3 October 2007. www.knbc.com/print/14265190/detail.html (accessed 4 October 2007).

Aaron, Susan. "Women with Badges." *FastWeb.* 2009. www.fastweb.com/ resources/articles/index/110245 (accessed 17 March 2009).

Abbott, Edith. "Training for the Policewoman's Job." *Woman Citizen.* April 1926. www.sameshield.com/press/sspress.35.html (accessed 26 May 2008).

*Adams v. Nolan,* 962 F.2d 791.

Albiston, Barbara. "Crime Fighting 'Mothers.'" *Bulletin.* March 2001, 3.

Alesia, Mark. "Patrick on Win: Women 'Capable of Anything.'" *Indianapolis Star.* 22 April 2008, 1(A).

Alfieri, Renee. "Human Relations Internship with the New York City Police Department." *Empowering Inquiry.* 2008. www.empoweringinquiry.com/ nypd3.html (accessed 18 March 2009).

"American Morning with Paula Zahn." *CNN.com.* 21 February 2002. http:// transcripts.cnn.com/TRANSCRIPTS/0202/21/ltm.06.html (accessed 1 June 2009).

Ax, Joseph. "Teaneck Settles Suits for $4.9M." *NorthJersey.com.* 30 April 2009. www.northjersey.com/news/crimeandcourts/Teaneck_settles_suits_ for_49M.html (accessed 4 May 2009).

Baker, Thomas E. and Jane P. Baker. "Preventing Police Suicide." *FBI Law Enforcement Bulletin*. October 1996, 24–27.

Barber, Karen, Kathy Miller, and Ellen Rosell. "Firefighting Women and Sexual Harassment." *Public Personnel Management* 24, no. 3 (September 1995): 339–50.

Barco, Mandalit del. "L.A. SWAT Unit on Verge of Accepting First Woman." *National Public Radio*. 14 June 2005. www.npr.org/templates/story/story.php?storyID=90015810 (accessed 3 May 2009).

Basich, Melanie. "Female Police Officers Must Walk a Fine Line Between Fitting in and Making Their Own Way in Law Enforcement." *Police*. June 2008. www.policemag.com/Articles/2008/06/Women-Warriors-1.aspx (accessed 12 March 2009).

Beardsley, Craig. "Women in Law Enforcement." *Indianapolis Magazine*. April 1976, 37–43.

*Berkman v. City of New York*, 672 F.2d 899.

Besecker, Aaron. "Stress Seen Hitting Female Police Officers Most." *Buffalo News*. 29 December 2008. www.buffalonews.com/cityregion/story/534938.html (accessed 17 March 2009).

Bloch, Peter B. and Deborah Anderson. *Policewomen on Patrol: Final Report*. Washington, DC: Police Foundation, 1974.

Brownlow, Louis. "The Policewoman's Sphere." *National Municipal Review*. March 1928. www.sameshield.com/press/sspress106.html (accessed 26 May 2008).

Bryce, Erin. "North Port Remembers Michele." *Sarasota Herald Tribune*. 15 July 2006, 8(B).

Canavor, Natalie. "Being One of the Guys Is Not a Chief Concern for One of Nassau County's First Policewomen." *Long Island Business News*. 9 June 2006.

Caruso, Michelle. "Fuhrman Led 'Klan' vs. Female Officers on Tapes, O.J. Trial Cop Tells of 'Tribunals.'" *New York Daily News*. 28 April 1997.

Cawdrey, John C. "Constance E (Connie) Worland." *The Backup: Newsletter of the California Reserve Peace Officers Association*. Summer 2006, 2.

Charles, Michael T. "Performance and Socialization of Female Recruits in the Michigan State Police Training Academy." *Journal of Police Science and Administration* 10, no. 1 (1981): 209–23.

———. "Women in Policing: The Physical Aspect." *Journal of Police Science and Administration* 10, no. 2 (1982): 194–205.

Cho, Cynthia H. "Policewoman Breaks the Brass Ceiling." *Los Angeles Times*. 28 March 2006. http://articles.latimes.com/2006/mar/28/local/me-chief28 (accessed 11 March 2008).

Coulter, Ann. "Freeze! I Just Had My Nails Done!" anncoulter.com. 16 March 2005. www.anncoulter.com/cgi-local/article.cgi?article=46 (accessed 7 June 2009).

"Department of State Seeks to Recruit Police Women for International Civilian Police Mission." Department of State Media Note. 29 June 2007.

Dernocoeur, Kate and James N. Eastman. "Have We Really Come a Long Way? Women in EMS Survey Results." *Journal of Emergency Medical Services* 17 (1992): 18–19.

"Dothan's First Female Officer Retires." *4WTVY*. 21 December 2006. www.wtvynews4.com/home/headlines/4985226.html (accessed 17 March 2009).

*Dothard v. Rawlinson*, 433 U.S. 321, 97 S.Ct. 2720.

Eaton, Leslie. "Officer's Slaying Leaves New Orleans Asking Why." *New York Times*. 31 January 2008. www.nytimes.com/2008/01/31/us/31shooting.html (accessed 20 May 2008).

Ebbert, Stephanie. "Under Hillman, Troopers Alleged Bias." *Boston Globe*. 9 March 2006.

Edmiston, Susan. "Policewomen: How Well Are They Doing a Man's Job?" *Ladies Home Journal*. April 1975, 126.

"The Effective Policewoman: A Study Program." *Woman's Journal*. May 1931. www.sameshield.com/press/sspress107.html (accessed 26 May 2008).

Eisenberg, Adam C. "The First Nine—Lure of Equal Pay Changed SPD Culture Forever." *Seattle Post Intelligencer/Seattle Times*. 28 October 2001, 4(D).

Fahy, Joe. "Pioneer Policewoman to Retire." *Indianapolis News*. 29 April 1989, 1(C).

"Famous Policewoman Urges Prevention of Crime." *New York Times*. 22 December 1912, 13(SM).

"Federal Law Enforcement Officers, 2002." U.S. Department of Justice—Bureau of Justice Statistics, NCJ-199995. August 2003, 7.

"Female Mounties Don't Feel Respected, Poll Finds." *RCMP Watch*. 29 October 2007. www.rcmpwatch.com/female-mounties-dont-feel-respected-poll-finds/ (accessed 17 March 2009).

"Female Officers in Knoxville Are Ordered to Cut Their Hair." *New York Times*. 26 October 1981, 13(A).

"Female Officers Win Suit against Nassau Police." WCBSTV. 17 November 2008. http://wcbstv.com/topstories/gener.discrimination.nassau.2.867074.html (accessed 18 March 2009).

"Female Police Officer Shot Dead." *Guardian Unlimited*. 19 November 2005.

"First Female Firefighter." *Arlington Fire Journal*. 18 March 2005. http://arlingtonfirejournal.blogspot.com/2005/03/first-female-firefighter.html (accessed 25 March 2009).

"First Female Officer Promoted to Deputy Chief." *Los Angeles Police Beat* 46, no. 7, July 2000, 1.

Folsom, Chandra Niles. "Women Advancing in Police Work, But Few Pursue It." *PoliceApp.com.* April 2008. www.policeapp.com/JusticeJournal/News View.asp?NewsId=16 (accessed 18 March 2009).

Foster, Keith. "Gender and Excessive Force Complaints." *Law and Order.* August 2006. www.hendonpub.com/resources/articlearchive/details .aspx?ID=764 (accessed 12 March 2009).

Fruits, Bettie. "Women 'Cops' Launch Squad Car Duty." *Indianapolis News.* 13 September 1968.

Gale, Mary Ellen. "Calling in the Girl Scouts: Feminist Legal Theory and Police Misconduct." *Loyola of Los Angeles Law Review* 34, no. 1 (2001): 691–747.

Gallo, Gina. "A Family Affair." *Police.* February 2005, 36–40.

Garcia, Venessa. "'Difference' in the Police Department." *Journal of Contemporary Criminal Justice* 19, no. 3 (August 2003): 330–44.

Gardiner, Sean. "Moira Ann Smith." *Newsday.* 13 February 2002. http://cf.newsday.com/911/victimsearch.cfm?id=423 (accessed 20 June 2008).

"Girls and Khaki." *Survey Graphic.* 1 December 1917. www.sameshield.com/press/sspress09c.html (accessed 26 May 2008).

Gonsoulin, Sheryl and C. Eddie Palmer. "Gender Issues and Partner Preferences among a Sample of Emergency Medical Technicians." *Prehospital and Disaster Medicine* 13, no. 1 (1997): 41–47.

Grant, Susan. "Dating a Female Cop." *Officer.com.* 8 July 2008. www.officer.com/publication/printer.jsp?id=29618 (accessed 16 March 2009).

———. "When Cops Marry Cops." *Officer.com.* 8 July 2008. www.officer.com/publication/printer.jsp?id=32856 (accessed 25 May 2009).

Griffith, Stephanie. "Few Women Follow Virginia's Trailblazing Firefighter." *Washington Post.* 25 December 1990, 1(PC).

Halbfinger, David M. "A Black Woman Sits in Bull Connor's Seat." *New York Times.* 3 May 2003, 12(A).

Halkova, Jarka. "Policewomen Seem to Be Winning the Fight for Acceptance." *Czech Radio.* 8 December 2005. www.radio.cz/en/article/73525 (accessed 11 March 2009).

Hamilton, Melanie. "Ballistic Vest Manufacturers Are Finding New Ways to Meet Female Officers' Needs." *Police.* October 2007, 31–36

Harrington, Penny E. and Kimberly Lonsway. "Current Barriers and Future Promise for Women in Policing." In *The Criminal Justice System and Women*, 3rd ed., edited by Barbara R. Price and Natalie J. Sokoloff. New York: McGraw-Hill, 2004, 495–510.

———. "Equality Denied, The Status of Women in Policing: 2000." The National Center for Women & Policing. Beverly Hills, CA, 2000, 3.

Helmer, Jodi. "Blazing the Trail." *Nervy Girl.* September/October 2002. www.sameshield.com/press/sspress129.html (accessed 26 May 2008).

Herbert, Keith. "Malverne Welcomes First Female Police Officer." *Newsday.* 11 July 2007.

Hill, Kim Quaile and Michael Clawson. "The Health Hazards of Street Level Bureaucracy: Mortality among the Police." *Journal of Police Science* 16, no. 4 (1988): 243–48.

Hillenmeyer, Katy. "Top Female Officer to Oversee Jail Expansion." *Press Democrat.* 5 June 2007, 1(A).

"Hiring and Retaining More Women." National Center for Women & Policing. Spring 2003. www.womenandpolicing.org/pdf/NewAdvantagesReport.pdf (accessed 17 March 2009).

Hoffman, Peter B. and Edward R. Hickey. "Use of Force by Female Police Officers." *Journal of Criminal Justice* 33, no. 2 (2005): 145–51.

Hoover, Larry T. "Trends in Police Physical Ability Selection Testing." *Public Personnel Management* 21, no. 1 (1992): 29–40.

Horne, Peter. "Policewomen: Their First Century and the New Era." *Police Chief.* September 2006, 23–32.

———. *Women in Law Enforcement.* Springfield, IL: Thomas, 1980.

Horne, Polly. "A Comparison of the Attitudes of Male Police Officers toward Female Police Officers from 1976 to 1994." 1995. www.fdle.state.fl.us/Content/getdoc/a68d0fd7-2cb3-4236-a378-81005626dd34/horne2.aspx (accessed 13 March 2009).

"How Male, Female Officers Manage Stress May Accentuate Stress on the Job." *Medical News Today.* 28 February 2009. www.medicalnewstoday.com/articles/140610.php (accessed 12 March 2009).

Howie, Michael. "Scotland's First Female Chief Constable to Lead Fife Force." *The Scotsman.* 7 June 2008. http://news.scotsman.com/lawandorder/Scotland39s-first-woman-chief-constable.4162254.jp (accessed 21 August 2009).

Hutzel, Eleanor. "The Policewoman." *The Annals of the American Academy of Political and Social Science.* November 1929. www.sameshield.com/press/sspress119.html (accessed 26 May 2008).

———. "The Policewoman's Role in Social Protection." *Journal of Social Hygiene.* December 1944. www.sameshield.com/press/sspress126.html (accessed 26 May 2008).

Johnson, Allen Jr. "The Legacy of Officer Cotton." *New Orleans Magazine.* 1 April 2008. www.neworleansmagazine.com/a/news/the-legacy-of-officer-cotton (accessed 20 May 2008).

"Justice Department Announces Court Decision that Eire, Pennsylvania Police Officer Test Discriminates against Women." U.S. Justice Department Press Release. 14 December 2005.

"Justice Department Sues Mississippi City Alleging Discrimination against a Female Lieutenant." U.S. Justice Department Press Release. 16 October 1996.

Kandaswamy, Deepa. "Indian Policewomen Practice Policing and Politicking." *Ms.* Winter 2004.

Kauffman, Ingrid. "Profile: Judith Brewer." *Arlington Sun Gazette.* 18 January 2001.

Keating, Thomas R. "Policewomen Manning Patrol Car." *Indianapolis Star.* 11 September 1968.

Keith, Kelly and Charlotte Kratchmer. "Train Women Separately from Men. *Law and Order.* June 2007. www.hendonpub.com/resources/articlearchive/details.aspx?ID=1291 (accessed 12 March 2009).

Kellner, Chelsea. "Female Officers Put up Long Fight for Acceptance." *Associated Press.* 11 March 2009.

———. "Wilmington's First Female Cop Put up Long Fight for Acceptance." *StarNewsOnLine.* 8 March 2009. www.starnewsonline.com/article/20090308/ARTICLES/903072970?Title=Wilmington-s-first-female-cop-put-up-long-fight-for-acceptance (accessed 15 August 2009).

King, Andrea. "SWAT Graduates First Female Officer." *Journal.* 14 September 2006. www.journalgroup.com/Belleville/1123/swat-graduates-first-female-officer (accessed 16 March 2009).

Knop, Laurie. "Woman Paramedic Pioneer." *Emergency* 7 (1977): 39–43.

Kunzelman, Michael. "Hundreds Mourn Slain Policewoman." WWLTV.com. 1 February 2008. www.wwltv.com/local/stories/wwl020108tpmourners.7d5b2876.html# (accessed 6 September 2009).

*Lanning v. SEPTA*, 308 F.3d 286.

"LAPD Working to Get More Female Officers." *Los Angeles Times.* 30 May 2003. www.sameshield.com/news/lapd.html (accessed 18 March 2009).

Lat, Emelyn Cruz. "Female Officers Furious at Firemen." *Seattle Times.* 25 April 1996.

Leger, Kristen. "Public Perceptions of Female Police Officers on Patrol." *American Journal of Criminal Justice* 21, no. 2 (March 1997): 231–49.

Lei, Owen. "Female Firefighter Wins Suit against Vashon Island FD." *King 5 News.* 12 February 2009. www.king5.com/news/local/60054812.html (accessed 1 June 2009).

Lennis, Susan. "Guys Will Ride in Car 47 Anytime . . . Cause the Fuzz Are Feminine." *Indianapolis Star Magazine.* 27 June 1971, 7–11.

Limon, Iliana. "Victory a Hollow One for Female Officer." *Albuquerque Tribune*. 26 November 2002, 1(A).

"Living Tribute to Yamel Merino." *Living Tributes*. 2009. http://livingtributes.com/livingtribute.php?memid=836 (accessed 2 June 2009).

Longa, Lyda. "Female Cops Love Their Careers." *News-Journal*. 1 March 2009. www.news-journalonline.com/NewsJournalOnline/News/Local/new EAST02030109.htm (accessed 17 March 2009).

Lynem, Julie N. "Female Officers Make Strides in Police Work." *Indianapolis Star*. 27 October 1996, 1(A).

Magrini, Kathy. "Town Holding Street Dedication to Honor Captain Kathy Mazza-Delosh." *Massapequa Post*. 9 October 2002, 1(A).

Malkin, Michelle. "What's Wrong with This Picture?" michellemalkin.com. 12 March 2005. http://michellemalkin.com/2005/03/12/whats-wrong-with-this-picture/ (accessed 26 April 2009).

Martin, Susan E. *Doing Justice, Doing Gender*. Thousand Oaks, CA: Sage, 2006.

———. "Women on the Move?" *Police Foundation Reports*. May 1989, 2.

McMahon, Susan. "Pelham's First Female Officer Welcomes Challenge." *Lowell Sun Online*. 28 June 2001. www.uml.edu/Media/News%20Articles/article124.html (accessed 16 March 2009).

*McNamara v. City of Chicago*, 853 F.2d 572.

"Men, Women, and Excessive Force." The National Center for Women & Policing. April 2002. www.womenandpolicing.org/PDF/2002_Excessive_Force.pdf (accessed 12 March 2009).

Mijares, Tomas C. "Selecting Police Personnel for Tactical Assignments: Considerations for Female Officers." *Applied H.R.M. Research* 4, no. 2 (1993): 94–101.

Miller, Susan L. *Gender and Community Policing: Walking the Talk*. Lebanon, NH: Northeastern University Press, 1999.

Montejo, Karin. "Success Factors of Women Who Have Achieved Positions of Command in Law Enforcement." Ph.D. diss., Lynn University, Boca Raton, FL, 2008.

Mroz, Jacqueline. "Female Police Chiefs, a Novelty No More." *New York Times*. 6 April 2008.

"My Son Hates the Idea of Me Becoming a Policewoman." *Gardenweb.com*. 13 December 2001. http://ths.gardenweb.com/forums/load/parents/msg1212231629555.html (accessed 3 December 2009).

The National Center for Women & Policing. *Recruiting & Retaining Women: A Self-Assessment Guide for Law Enforcement*. Los Angeles: The National Center for Women & Policing, 2000.

Nelson, Josephine. "On the Policewoman's Beat." *Independent Woman*. May 1936. www.sameshield.com/press/sspress112.html (accessed 26 May 2008).

Newman, Andy. "Town Rejects Female Officer." *New York Times*. 28 February 1997, 1(B).

"No Charges to Be Filed in F.B.I. Agent's Death." *New York Times*. 12 October 1985.

"Number of Full-Time Law Enforcement Employees by Agency as of October 31, 2007." www.dps.state.ia.us/commis/ucr/2007/2007_UCR_Table_LE.pdf (accessed 29 June 2009).

"Officer Down: Characteristics of Cop Killings." *The Forensic Examiner*. 22 March 2008.

Penney, John. "Q & A with Donna Ash Brown, Putnam's First Female Police Officer." *Norwich Bulletin*. 10 December 2008.

"Pennsylvania Governor Rendell Announces New, Customized State Police Mobile Recruiting Office." Press release from the Office of the Governor of Pennsylvania, 5 June 2003.

Perin, Michelle. "So, You Want to Date a Female Cop?" *Officer.com*. 10 March 2009. www.officer.com/web/online/Police-Life/So-You-Want-to-Date-a-Female-Cop/17$45721 (accessed 16 March 2009).

Pettus, Takesha. "Three Officers, Including First Female, Join SRPD." *Sentinel*. 26 July 2000, 1(A).

Pigeon, Helen D. "Policewomen and Public Recreation." *The American City*. October 1927. www.sameshield.com/press/sspress128.html (accessed 26 May 2008).

"Police Matrons." *Harper's Weekly*. August 1890. www.sameshield.com/press/sspress01.html (accessed 26 May 2008).

"Policewoman Moira Smith." *Scottish Daily Record*. 11 September 2002. www.womenatgroundzero.com/Pages/GlasgowRecord.html (accessed 20 May 2008).

"Policewoman Mourned." *Indianapolis News*. 25 September 1974, 4.

"A Policewoman on Trial." *Survey Graphic*. 15 April 1922. www.sameshield.com/press/sspress13.html (accessed 26 May 2008).

"Policewomen Manning Patrol Car." *Police Journal*. Fall 1968, 37.

"Portland Blacks Outraged by 'Sleeper-Hold' T-Shirts." *Eugene Register-Guard*. 30 April 1985, 5(A).

The President's Commission on Law Enforcement and the Administration of Justice. *The Challenge of Crime in a Free Society*. Washington, DC: U.S. Government Printing Office, 1967.

Pridemore, Amelia A. "Percentage of W.Va. Female Police Officers in Single Digits." *Register-Herald.* 24 January 2009. www.register-herald.com/local/local_story_024232858.html (accessed 13 March 2009).

"Profiles of Leadership: Bonni G. Tischler." *The Business of Government.* Spring 2001. www.sameshield.com/press/sspress124.html (accessed 26 May 2008).

Reaves, Brian A. "Local Police Departments 1993." U.S. Department of Justice—Bureau of Justice Statistics, NCJ-148822. April 1996, iii.

Roman, Alex. "Female Police Officers Are a Minority and Their Uniform Needs Have Largely Been Ignored by the Market; but That's Changing." *Police.* December 2005. www.policemag.com/Print/Articles/2005/12/The-Other-10-Percent.aspx (accessed 12 March 2009).

Ross, Albert Jr. "Female Officers Are Rare Sight in Area's Police Departments." *Augusta Chronicle.* 2 June 2003. http://chronicle.augusta.com/stories/060203/met_070-8069.000.shtml (accessed 17 March 2009).

Rossi, Adam T. "Progress of Female Officers." *Saratoga Today.* 29 February 2008. www.saratoga.com/today/2008/02/progress-of-female-officers.html (accessed 12 March 2009).

Salazar, Denisse. "Pepper Spray and Endless Pushups Is What It Took." *Orange County Register.* 3 April 2008.

"San Jose Police Struggle to Recruit, Retain Female Officers." *Mercury News.* 29 May 2002.

Sauls, John Gales. "Proving Business Necessity: The Disparate Impact Challenge." *Lectlaw.* April 1995. www.lectlaw.com/files/emp35.htm (accessed 8 May 2009).

Scheer, Robert. "Joseph Wambaugh: What LAPD Needs Is Women to Combat Testosterone Level." *Los Angeles Times.* 14 July 1991, 3(M).

Schnepp, Marilyn. "My Friend Shanty." *Faith Writers.* 16 August 2006. www.faithwriters.com/article-details.php?id=49572 (accessed 20 June 2008).

Segrave, Kerry. *Policewomen: A History.* Jefferson, NC: McFarland & Company, 1995.

"Sexual Harassment in the Fire Service." International Association of Women in Fire & Emergency Services. 2008. www.i-women.org/issues.php?issue=3 (accessed 15 March 2009).

Shaughnessy, John J. "Policewomen Chalk Up String of Firsts." *Indianapolis Star.* 1 August 1982, 1(B).

"She Still Insists on Policewomen." *New York Times.* 31 March 1907. www.sameshield.com/press/sspress01a.html (accessed 26 May 2008).

Shpritzer, Felicia. "A Case for the Promotion of Policewomen in the City of New York." *Journal of Criminal Law, Criminology, and Police Science* 50, no. 4 (November–December 1959): 415–19.

Silvers, Amy Rabideau. "Estrada Blazed Trail for Other Officers." *Milwaukee Journal Sentinel*, 25 August 2006.

Smith, Bertha H. "The Policewoman." *Good Housekeeping.* March 1911, 22–25.

Smith, James Walter. "Enter the Lady Cops of Gotham." *Boston Evening Transcript.* 18 May 1918. www.sameshield.com/press/sspress09aa.html (accessed 26 May 2008).

Smothers, Ronald. "At Work with: Beverly Harvard." *New York Times.* 30 November 1994, 1(C).

Snow, Robert L. *SWAT Teams: Explosive Face-Offs with America's Deadliest Criminals.* New York: Perseus, 1999.

Sousa, William and Jane Florence Gauthier. "Gender Diversity in Officers' Evaluations of Police Work." *Justice Policy Journal* 5, no. 1, Spring 2008. www.cjcj.org/files/gender_diversity.pdf (accessed 26 May 2009).

Stanhouse, Nick. "From Desk to Patrol Car." *The Indiana Trooper.* August 1979, 225–29.

Steel, Brent and Nicholas Lovrich. "Equality and Efficiency Tradeoffs in Affirmative Action—Real or Imagined?" *Social Science Journal* 24, no. 1 (1987): 53–70.

Steel, Brent S. and Rebecca L. Warner. "Affirmative Action in Times of Fiscal Stress and Changing Value Priorities: The Case of Women in Policing." *Public Personnel Management* 18 (Fall 1989): 291–309.

Stokes, Derrick. "Police Protection Is a Relative Matter." *Indianapolis News.* 18 March 1991, 1(C).

Tamber, Caryn. "Philly's First Female Cops Fought an Uphill Battle for Equality." *Daily Pennsylvanian.* 28 November 2000. http://thedp.com/node/21868 (accessed 27 May 2008).

"Tearing Down the Wall." National Center for Women & Policing. Spring 2003. www.pennyharrington.com/impactofagility.htm (accessed 7 May 2009).

Terpstra, David E. and R. Bryan Kethley. "Organizations' Relative Degree of Exposure to Selection Discrimination Litigation." *Public Personnel Management* 31, no. 3 (2002): 277–92.

*Thomas v. City of Evanston*, 610 F.Supp. 422,431 (N.D. Ill. 1985).

Thompson B., A. Kirk-Brown, and A. Brown. "Police Women and Their Partners: Influence and Outcomes of Work Stress in the Family." Paper presented at the Australasian Conference of Women and Policing, Brisbane, Australia, July 1999.

"Today in San Francisco History." *Sfist.* 2008. http://sfist.com/2008/12/09/ today_in_san_francisco_history_miss.php (accessed 11 March 2009).

*UAW v. Johnson Controls, Inc.,* 499 U.S.187 (1991).

"Uniform Crime Reports." www.fbi.gov/ucr/ucr.htm (accessed 29 June 2009).

"United States Attorney Joseph P. Russoniello Announces Appointment of Annemarie Conroy as Law Enforcement Coordinator." U.S. Justice Department Press Release. 24 April 2008.

"United States Census 2000." www.census.gov/main/www/cen2000.html (accessed 27 February 2009).

Van Winkle, Mina C. "The Policewoman." *Survey Graphic.* 24 September 1924. www.sameshield.com/press/sspress21.html (accessed 26 May 2008).

Vollmer, August. "Meet the Lady Cop." *Survey Graphic.* 15 March 1930. www .sameshield.com/press/sspress104.html (accessed 26 May 2008).

———. "The Policewoman and Pre-Delinquency." *Woman Citizen.* March 1926. www.sameshield.com/press/sspress34.html (accessed 26 May 2008).

Wamuyu, Ruth C. "Three Female Officers Work for UPD." *Spartan Daily.* 26 October 2004. www.sjsupd.com/pages/news/102604.html (accessed 18 March 2009).

Waugh, Alec. "Women in Policing." Paper presented at the Australian Institute of Criminology Conference, Sydney, Australia, 29 July 1996.

Whetstone, Muriel L. "Atlanta's Top Cop—Police Chief Beverly J. Harvard." *Ebony.* March 1995, 92–95.

———. "The Nation's First Black Woman Sheriff: Jackie Barrett." *Ebony.* August 1995.

Wicker, Tom. "Police Troubles Know No Gender." *Spokesman-Review.* 2 May 1985, 4(A).

Willis, Justin. "Owensboro, Ky., Police Department Seeks to Increase Number of Female Officers." *Messenger-Inquirer.* 2 February 2003.

Wilson, O. W. *Police Administration.* Columbus, OH: McGraw-Hill, 1963.

"Women Become Policemen as Police Become Soldiers." *American City.* April 1943. www.sameshield.com/press/sspress118.html (accessed 26 May 2008).

"Women in the LAPD." *LAPDonline.* 2008. www.lapdonline.org/ history_of_ the_lapd/content_basic_view/833 (accessed 12 June 2008).

"Women on Patrol?" *Indianapolis News.* 16 September 1968.

"Women Police of Detroit." *New York Times.* 13 March 1921, 4(sec 9).

Zamora, Jim Herron. "Study Finds Cops Twice as Likely to Abuse Family." *San Francisco Examiner.* 17 November 1997, 1(A).

# INDEX

# ABOUT THE AUTHOR

**Robert L. Snow** served on the Indianapolis Police Department for thirty-eight years, retiring in 2007 with the rank of captain. While at the police department he held such positions as police department executive officer, captain of detectives, and commander of the homicide branch. He is also the author of more than a dozen books, including *Looking for Carroll Beckwith, Murder 101,* and *Deadly Cults.*